D0297489

I TOLD YOU
I WAS ILL

I TOLD YOU
I WAS ILL

MARIA PRITCHARD

RW PRESS

Contents

Introduction

As Woody Allen (pictured) once said, 'I'm not afraid to die, I just don't want to be there when it happens.' Allen's quip may reflect how many of us feel about 'checking out' but as the only certainty of life, death is a fascinating subject and can also be devastatingly funny. Laughter is often a way of dealing with the more difficult aspects of life. Some wits, like Woody Allen, make a career of using humour to explore the Really Big Subjects and death is no exception. It is only natural that some will use humour as a way of saying goodbye and ensuring they are remembered with a smile.

Not all last words are humorous, however. Some are profound and others poetic; some are heart-rending, such as John Belushi's 'Just don't leave me alone.' Some clearly anticipate what is about to befall them, whereas others appear hopelessly mistaken, such as Caligula's 'I live!' Some express noble sentiments and others disillusionment, with Winston Churchill and Kenneth Williams providing withering examples of a downbeat exit. Some departees were clearly too surprised by the unexpected turn of events to offer anything other than a statement of the obvious, as in 'I'm shot.' Mark Twain, who put such great store by wit and last words, was cut short by the grim reaper, silenced mid-sentence, probably depriving us of one last glittering remark.

Some of the best epilogues come from those aware of their impending fate. Convicts facing execution might therefore be expected to deliver the best closing speeches: they have the dubious advantage of knowing the exact time of their death and usually have plenty of opportunity beforehand to contemplate their exit. However, this cohort's last words often fall short. Some chose to exit with dreadful puns, some showed remorse but a large contingent go unrepentant. Few display any great wisdom, perhaps an indication of how they arrived at their situation in the first place.

Conversely, expecting someone to deliver the perfect *bons mots* at a time when they are probably not quite at their best seems like a tall order. It is hardly surprising that so many get it wrong. Even those renowned for their wisdom can fail at the crucial moment. Socrates, the great thinker and arguably the father of Western philosophy, had taken his leave of the assembly which sentenced him to death with words fit for posterity: 'It is now time to leave – for me to die and for you to live – though which of us has the better destiny is unclear to everyone, save only to God.' If only he had left it at this. It seems even great philosophers are prone to distraction by the more prosaic concerns of life. His actual last words, before the Hemlock's poison finally silenced him forever, were addressed to his friend: 'Crito, we owe a cock to Aesculapius; please pay it and don't let it pass'. As seen in Mark Twain's example, timing is of the essence.

The deathbed may be somewhere people can express themselves freely: they have nothing to lose or to gain. It may be the final chance to unburden a guilty soul by confessions of guilt or the revelation of long-held secrets. The words of the soon-to-be-departed may reveal what really matters once the chips are down, a statement of longing for the most cherished things in life, such as Napoleon Bonaparte's list of 'France, Army, Josephine. ' In other cases, it is the simpler things that evoke regret, as in Kit Carson's wistful comment, 'I wish I had time for one more bowl of chilli.'

It is perhaps not surprising that writers, actors and politicians make up the largest number quoted here – people for whom words, both written and spoken, are the main currency. It is also conspicuous that the majority of quotations come from white men: traditionally the possessors of the fame and power necessary to make their last words considered worth recording (or inventing).

So why do last words hold such a fascination? Many of us are curious about how others have dealt with the final task of ceasing to be. It can be intriguing to discover whether familiar personalities stayed true to type as they took their last breaths: did the hero remain brave and resolute? Did the wisecracking comedienne retain her sense of humour? This book will reveal that in many cases, last words do fit our image of the recently departed. For some, a sense of humour seems almost the last thing to go, with death providing the perfect opportunity to deliver a punch line. A few, such as Leslie Nielsen, were so determined to be remembered with glee, they left instructions for their gravestones to be inscribed with a joke.

Finally, a note of caution should be expressed. Many of these epitaphs are of dubious veracity and even some of the best known should be taken with a pinch of salt. In several cases, the quotations are apocryphal. Some individuals have acquired more than one epitaph and some epitaphs have been attributed to more than one person. This suggests how important the convention of The Last Words is. Pancho Villa seemed to recognize this when he asked his companion to 'Tell them I said something.' He apparently understood that the final statement is an important part of a character's myth and crucial for any hero (although Villa's quotation is itself of dubious provenance.) Last words may be part of the mythologizing process, putting a final, gratifying touch to our image of the deceased. It seems fitting, perhaps even reassuring, that someone as relentlessly witty as Groucho Marx should leave life with a quip. Those who retain a sense of humour in the face of death are particularly admirable. Some may yearn for a deeper wisdom, inspired by the proximity of the great unknown. There have certainly been many poetic and profound statements but the more sceptical in nature may find these particularly suspect. Not all last words are questionable, however. Some were noted in written form, others had several corroborating witnesses and a few have even been recorded on film. Modern technology provides efficient means of communication and new methods of conveying last words have begun to appear, with Tweets and texts already delivering some final thoughts.

This collection will reveal just about every approach that has been taken by the eminent and the notorious to their ultimate utterance.

THAT'S ALL FOLKS!

Actors, Comedians and the Entertainment Business

'I told you I was ill'

Spike Milligan,1918 – 2002. Born in India to an English mother and Irish father, Terence Alan Patrick Sean Milligan became one of the best-loved comedic actors and writers in Britain. He was part of the innovative and influential *The Goon Show*, along with Peter Sellers and Harry Secombe, wrote and starred in his own television shows, and appeared in Monty Python's *The Life of Brian*. Spike was also a musician, artist, an environmental campaigner and spoke publicly about his bipolarism. He died of kidney failure at his home in East Sussex.

A celebrated eccentric, Spike was often outspoken. However, his family could not agree whether he had been joking when he said he wanted the inscription 'I told you I was ill' on his gravestone. For two years after his death, his grave lacked a headstone until a compromise was finally reached: the joke would be included – but in Gaelic. It now reads 'Duirt me leat go raibh me breoite' below the English inscription 'Love, light, peace'.

....

'Let 'er rip'

Leslie Nielsen,1926 – 2010. Nielsen was born in Saskatchewan, Canada, to a Danish father and a Welsh mother. He appeared in more than 50 films as well as numerous television series, such as *Police Squad*. Although he had always been drawn to comedy, most of his long career was spent playing 'serious' parts. When he finally appeared in a comedy role (in *Airplane!*), it made him a huge star. He died in Florida, of complications from pneumonia. His family said he simply fell asleep and passed away peacefully. Although his last words are not recorded, the epitaph on his tombstone paid homage to his notorious love of 'fart gags'.

'I've never felt better.'

Douglas Fairbanks, 1883 – 1939. The swashbuckling star of many silent movies, suffered a fatal heart attack in 1939 but even this did not seem to dent his style. He found fame in early action adventures such as *The Mark of Zorro* and *Robin Hood*. However, he was not only a talented performer but also showed good business sense by co-founding United Artists and the Motion Picture Academy, who are responsible for awarding Oscars. The arrival of 'talking pictures' effectively put an end to his acting career, although he did not retire from acting until 1934.

....

'Just don't leave me alone.'

John Belushi, 1949 – 1982. The American actor, comedian and musician first made his name in the television show *Saturday Night Live*, going on to star in hit movies such as *The Blues Brothers* and *Animal House*. He earned a reputation for wild living and hard drinking but it was a 'speedball', an injected mix of heroin and cocaine, which was cited as the cause of death. On the night of 4 March 1982, Belushi had been partying in his rooms at the Chateau Marmont in Los Angeles. He was found dead the next morning, alone in bed. Some months later Cathy Smith, an acquaintance of Belushi's, admitted in an interview with *Rolling Stone* that she had given him the fatal speedball. This public admission resulted in her arrest and she was convicted of involuntary manslaughter, serving 15 months in prison.

Belushi's original tombstone read, 'I may be gone but Rock and Roll lives on.' His burial plot became a magnet to many of his fans, some of whom desecrated the grave and marred the surrounding area. Consequently, at his widow's request, his remains were moved to a secret, unmarked site.

'Please don't leave me. Please don't leave me.'

Chris Farley, 1964 – 1997. Like his idol John Belushi, Farley made his name on *Saturday Night Live*. Also like his idol, Farley was addicted to drink and drugs and probably died after taking a speedball. He had spent the day with a prostitute called Heidi, smoking crack and snorting heroin. When she left at 3 a.m., Farley was in bad shape. After begging her not to leave, he collapsed near the doorway. Although he seemed to be having difficulty breathing, she just took a photograph of him lying on the floor and left. His brother found him on the same spot the following afternoon. He called the paramedics who pronounced him dead at the scene. Farley had once said he '…dreamed of being John Belushi…I wanted to follow him.' Like Belushi, he was just 33 years old when he died.

......

'It was the food! Don't touch the food!'

Richard Harris, 1930 – 2002. This was a last prank from Harris. He called out the warning to hotel guests as paramedics wheeled him through a hotel foyer, taking him to hospital for cancer treatment. The Irish actor, director, singer, producer and writer was renowned for his hell-raising and his wit. Born in Limerick, he was largely self-educated and moved to London to study acting. After being nominated for an Oscar, he became a major Hollywood star of films including *The Heroes of Telelmark* and *A Man Called Horse*. His drinking style was also epic until he was given the last rites during one particularly impressive binge; he subsequently gave up alcohol. One of his last roles was that of Albus Dumbledore in the first two *Harry Potter* films. He died in hospital of Hodgkin's lymphoma.

'Die my dear? Why that's the last thing I'll do!'

Groucho Marx, 1890 – 1977. Possibly one of the funniest men of all time, Groucho was born Julius Henry Marx in New York City. Initially, he wanted to be a doctor but began appearing as a singer, encouraged by his 'stage mother' who wanted all of her five children to enter theatrical careers. It was only when the brothers turned to comedy, with Groucho giving vent to his rapid one-liners that they found success. Broadway hits soon became radio and then movie successes, although the pressures cost Groucho a mental breakdown. Following their break-up, Groucho wrote books and hosted game shows where he could exploit his quick-fire wit. His physical and mental health had long suffered before he finally succumbed to pneumonia at Cedars-Sinai Medical Centre in Los Angeles. Although these last words are probably apocryphal, many confirmed that Groucho retained his sense of humour to the end. Whilst on his deathbed, a nurse approached him saying she wanted to see if he had a temperature. 'Don't be silly,' he replied, 'everyone has a temperature.'

....

'Mom, I'm dying.'

Brittany Murphy, 1977 – 2009. The Atlanta-born actress began her career in theatre at just nine years old. She soon landed major roles in television shows and graduated to a starring role in the comedy film *Clueless* in 1995. Murphy was able to deliver not only comedy but serious dramatic performances. She died at her California home at the age of just 32 and her mother reportedly found her collapsed in the bathroom. She had suffered a cardiac arrest but the autopsy recorded the primary cause to be pneumonia, anemia and multiple drug intoxication. Her husband reported she had been taking a mixture of medicines to counter a respiratory infection and the coroner concurred that all of the drugs found in her system were legal but that the high amounts probably contributed to her death.

'It wasn't worth it.'

Louis B. Mayer, 1884 – 1957. This was a strangely downbeat ending for the film producer who ran Metro-Goldwyn-Mayer movies and was widely credited as the inventor of the Hollywood 'star system'. Mayer, often known simply as L.B., presided over some of the biggest stars of the 1930s and 1940s and was credited with discovering such luminaries as Joan Crawford, Greta Garbo, Clark Gable, Katherine Hepburn and Fred Astaire. He was something of a father figure to many of the actors and even gave Judy Garland away at her wedding to Vincent Minnelli. Away from the film business, Mayer was an extremely successful racehorse owner and breeder, building one of the finest stables in the United States of America. When he died of leukemia, 2,000 people gathered in the temple on Wilshire Boulevard, Los Angeles, for his memorial service with a further 3,000 waiting outside. Many stars, including Fred Astaire and James Stewart attended and Spencer Tracy delivered the eulogy. L.B. Mayer's life had been one of the classic, rags-to-riches stories of the American Dream.

....

'It's all been rather lovely.'

John Le Mesurier, 1912 – 1983. The mild-mannered British star was perhaps best known for the long-running television comedy *Dad's Army*. However, he also appeared in repertory theatre and many film and television productions. Although he reportedly never appeared drunk, he was a heavy drinker and died from a complication of cirrhosis of the liver. He spoke these last words to his wife, just before sinking into a final coma. He also wrote his own death notice for *The Times*, which read 'John Le Mesurier wishes it to be known that he conked out on November 15th. He sadly misses family and friends.'

'How slow my death agony is.'

Sarah Bernhardt, 1844 – 1923. After taking her theatre company on a world tour, the French actress became one of the first internationally renowned stars of the stage, even tackling some of the classic male roles, such as Hamlet. She was also one of the first actors to appear in the new medium of motion pictures. 'The Divine Sarah' had a volatile and eccentric nature: she reputedly slept in a coffin to enrich her interpretations of the great tragic roles. During the Franco-Prussian War, she converted her theatre to a hospital and temporarily gave up acting to tend wounded soldiers. Throughout World War I, she again visited soldiers on the front line, despite having lost a leg to gangrene. She was reportedly offered $10,000 (£6,200) for the display of her amputated leg, which she refused. It was said that the loss of her limb did not diminish her performances in any way, although she disliked using a prosthetic leg. She also painted and sculpted, wrote a novel, an autobiography and a treatise on acting. France awarded her the *Legion d'Honneur* in 1914. She died in Paris of uraemia and was buried at Pére-Lachaise cemetery.

....

'Yes, it's tough but not as tough as doing comedy.'

Edmund Gwen, 1877 – 1959. This was the British actor's response when asked whether dying was hard. He appeared in at least 80 films, including roles for George Cukor, Alfred Hitchcock and the Ealing Comedy Studios. Gwen won an Oscar for Best Supporting Actor for his portrayal of Santa Claus in *Miracle on 34th Street*. After suffering a stroke, he finally died of the resultant pneumonia. A similar quote is attributed to another British actor, Edmund Kean who died in 1833.

'I should never have switched from scotch to martinis.'

or

'Goodbye kid.'

Humphrey Bogart (pictured), 1899 – 1957. 'Bogie' was the great American star of such classic Hollywood films as *Casablanca*, *The Maltese Falcon* and *The Big Sleep*, with a career spanning nearly 30 years and 75 films. His public image was one of a tough-talking, hard-drinking man. In private, he was well read and a skilful sailor. However, he was also an innate rebel who enjoyed drinking, arguing and practical jokes. Bogart publicly organized opposition to the persecution of actors and screenwriters by the powerful House Un-American Activities Committee: a brave act during a time of almost hysterical paranoia in America.

Whilst filming *To Have and Have Not* in 1944, Bogart, at 44, met the 16-year-old Lauren Bacall. She was stunningly beautiful as well as funny and outspoken. Their affair brought Bogart's unhappy third marriage to an end and was the beginning of their life-long partnership. They married in 1945, had two children and made another three films together. By the mid 1950s, Bogart's heavy smoking and drinking had taken their toll and he was diagnosed with esophageal cancer. In typical 'Bogie' fashion, he refused to see a doctor until the disease was too advanced to be treatable. He died at his home and although his funeral service was simple by Hollywood standards, guests included James Mason, Katherine Hepburn, Judy Garland, Marlene Dietrich, Bette Davis and David Niven, among many other stars of the time. John Huston delivered the eulogy for his friend. The quote about Martinis is probably apocryphal. Bacall was the last to see him alive: she left the house to pick up their children and when she returned he had slipped into a coma from which he never recovered.

'Oh what's the bloody point?'

Kenneth Williams, 1926 – 1988. British comic actor and diarist, Williams achieved fame in Britain through the radio series *Round the Horne*, television appearances in *Hancock's Half Hour* and most widely in the *Carry On* series of films. However, he never reconciled his disappointment at not achieving recognition as a serious actor and was scathing in his diaries about the down-market *Carry On* films. His sexuality also seems to have caused him conflict. In his youth, homosexuality was still illegal so he was unable to be open about his true nature. Later, he seemed to have been celibate, at least from his 40s on and to have shrunk from intimacy of any kind. He lived next door to his mother but had few friends and apparently no romantic relationships. Williams was prone to depression which worsened as his loneliness grew and his health deteriorated. Finally, he took an overdose of barbiturates but as it was impossible to ascertain whether this had been accidental, the coroner recorded an open verdict. His often funny and acerbic diaries and letters were published posthumously, revealing the depths of his depression and suicidal thoughts. His last words come from the final entry in his diary, made the day before his death.

....

'I'm glad that's over.'

Eric Morecambe, 1926 – 1984. The much-loved British comedian was one half of the Morecambe and Wise double act which lasted over 40 years. The pair became a fixture of British Saturday evening peak-time television with their joyful and irreverent brand of humour. On the evening of his death, Morecambe had been performing solo at the Roses Theatre in Tewkesbury. At the show's finale, he took six curtain calls with the musicians but when he returned backstage, collapsed with a heart attack. Eric died a few hours later in hospital. He left a wife and three children as well as his comedy partner Ernie, who died in 1999.

'Why not? After all, it belongs to him.'

Charles 'Charlie' Chaplin, 1889 – 1977. The above was Chaplin's response to the priest who attended his deathbed with the phrase 'May the Lord have mercy on your soul.'

Born into poverty in South London, Chaplin became one of the first superstars of the silent movie era. Even today, the 'Little Tramp' remains one of the most iconic figures in film history and his perfectionism brought critical acclaim from the film industry. Although his brand of comedy was often sentimental and slapstick, he became more political in later films such as *The Great Dictator*.

Both of Chaplin's parents were music hall entertainers and his career began as a child performer on the British vaudeville stages. At 19 years old, he moved to America and began work in the nascent film industry with Mack Sennett and the Keystone Company. He not only acted but wrote, edited, directed, scored and produced most of his own films. The public adored him and he soon achieved stardom and adulation from all over the world. In the 1940s, Chaplin fell foul of the pervasive atmosphere of paranoia in the United States. He moved to Switzerland in 1952 to avoid investigation into his communist sympathies, as well as a protracted paternity suit.

Chaplin died of a stroke at his home in Switzerland on Christmas Day, 1977 and was buried near his home. A year after his death, his remains were stolen and held to ransom. However, his widow refused to pay, saying 'Charlie would have thought it ridiculous.' Within a few weeks the two bodysnatchers were arrested, Chaplin's body was recovered and reburied in a thief-proof concrete casement.

'Tape *Seinfeld* for me.'

Harvey Korman, 1927 – 2008. Korman became a familiar face on American television from the 1960s on, appearing in *The Carol Burnett Show*, *Ellen*, *ER* and *The Love Boat*. His particular gift was for comedy and he appeared in films such as *Blazing Saddles* and *Herbie Goes Bananas*. He died as a result of an abdominal aortic aneurysm at the UCLA Medical Centre.

....

'Codeine...bourbon...'

Tallulah Bankhead, 1902 – 1968. This American actress was born into a wealthy and politically prominent Alabama family. She became renowned for her acting as well as her loud, deep voice, larger-than-life personality and liberal ethics. The outspoken and quick-tempered Bankhead was extremely witty and had a highly colourful reputation about which she was candid. She once said, 'Only good girls keep diaries, bad girls don't have the time' and described herself as 'Pure as the driven slush.' She achieved success on both stage and screen but found the process of filmmaking boring, preferring the challenge of the theatre. In her later years, she worked successfully in American radio and television.

Her hearty enthusiasm for life included a 150-a-day cigarette habit, heavy drinking, a voracious sexual appetite as well as a love of baseball and legendary generosity. She famously joked, 'Cocaine isn't habit forming. I should know: I've been taking it for years.' Although undoubtedly keen on men, she was also rumoured to have had affairs with Greta Garbo, Marlene Dietrich and Billie Holliday, describing herself as 'ambisextrous'.

She died of double pneumonia in a New York hospital. She was also suffering emphysema, malnutrition and possibly a bout of Hong Kong influenza.

'Hello.'

or

'Sorry for saying f**k.'

Graham Chapman, 1941 – 1989. One of the internationally successful and enduringly influential *Monty Python* team of writers and actors, Chapman studied medicine at Cambridge University where he also met John Cleese and Eric Idle. The team valued his comedy acumen and eccentric outlook, as well as his acting abilities: he took the lead roles in the Monty Python films *The Life of Brian* and *Monty Python and the Holy Grail*. Outwardly, he may have appeared the traditional, educated Englishman: a tall, pipe-smoking enthusiast of rugby and mountaineering. However, he was also an alcoholic, struggling with an addiction which often compromised his work and frequently irritated his colleagues. Chapman was one of the first British celebrities to 'come out' publicly about his sexuality and became a spokesman for Gay rights. He was often referred to as the 'silliest of the Pythons' and was a founding member of the Dangerous Sports Club, partly responsible for introducing bungee jumping to Britain.

Chapman died from cancer of the throat and spine. He was attended by members of his family, his long-time partner and two members of the Python team. 'Hello' may have been his last comment, on seeing the arrival of his adopted son. The other comment was reportedly addressed to a nurse who had just accidentally stuck a needle into his arm. John Cleese and Michael Palin spoke at his funeral and Eric Idle led the gathering in a rendition of *Always Look on the Bright Side of Life* from *The Life of Brian*.

'Say goodbye to Pat, say goodbye to Jack and say goodbye to yourself, because you're a nice guy.'

Marilyn Monroe (pictured), 1926 – 1962. Born in Los Angeles into an unstable family life, Norma Jean would become the most iconic of American actresses and an archetypal sex symbol. She starred in numerous Hollywood hits including *Gentlemen Prefer Blondes*, *The Seven Year Itch* and *Some Like it Hot*. However, she longed to be taken seriously and to break free of the dumb blonde typecasting which pervaded her career. Many acquaintances remarked on her intelligence and sweet nature: qualities at odds with her public image. Despite her film success, her personal life was deeply unhappy, with three failed marriages, a miscarriage and prescription drug and alcohol dependencies providing a forlorn backdrop.

Her last comments concluded a telephone conversation with fellow actor Peter Lawford. 'Pat' probably referred to Patricia Kennedy Lawford; Peter Lawford's wife and sister of President John F. Kennedy. 'Jack' was President Kennedy, rumoured to have had an affair with Monroe. Marilyn died of barbiturate poisoning, probably in a suicide bid, although it is impossible to be certain whether it was intentional. Both her physical and mental health had become increasingly fragile and this had impacted on her work. 20th Century Fox had sacked her from her final film project and launched a lawsuit against her. However, this had been resolved and friends reported that in the week before her death, she was in good spirits and had never looked better.

Some of the conspiracy theories surrounding her death involve murder, the mafia and the Kennedys. However, Peter Lawford reported that during their final conversation, her speech was slurred making him concerned enough to telephone her housekeeper, asking that she check on Marilyn. Following her death, Joe DiMaggio, Marilyn's second husband, arranged to have red roses placed at her crypt three times a week for the next 20 years.

'Kurt Russell'

Walt Disney, 1901 – 1966. Even Kurt Russell doesn't understand this one. Walter Elias Disney was one of the giants of 20th century entertainment. The list of his activities in the film industry includes animation, direction, screenwriting and acting (providing the voices for animation). Under his direction, his studios created some of the most iconic animation figures such as Mickey Mouse. Following a lifetime of chain smoking, he died in hospital from lung cancer. He left a final note, containing just these two words: 'Kurt Russell'. Russell was only about 15 years old at the time but had already starred in a number of television series. After Disney's death, the actor was signed to the Walt Disney Company and became one of their top stars during the 1970s. The rumour that Walt Disney was cryogenically frozen is, disappointingly, unfounded: his body was cremated.

....

'Die? I should say not, dear fellow. No Barrymore would allow such a conventional thing to happen to him.'

John Barrymore, 1882 – 1942. This handsome stage and screen actor was a member of the talented and eccentric Barrymore acting dynasty; brother to Lionel and Ethel and grandfather to Drew. His career spanned silent movies and the talkies as well as roles ranging from light comedy to Shakespearean Tragedy. He collapsed whilst recording a radio show and died later in hospital with his brother and daughter at his side. According to Errol Flynn, a film director somehow acquired Barrymore's corpse and left it seated in a chair at Flynn's home, awaiting his return from a night's drinking. This story may be apocryphal as it re-appears in other scenarios and is denied by at least one of Barrymore's closest friends.

'Dear World, I'm leaving you because I'm bored. I feel I have lived long enough. I am leaving you with your worries in this sweet cesspool. Good luck.'

George Sanders, 1906 – 1972. The urbane British actor left this sentiment in a suicide note then took an overdose of sleeping pills. He was not only an Oscar-winning actor but a singer, songwriter, composer and author. He appeared in film classics such as *All About Eve* and Alfred Hitchcock's *Rebecca* as well as providing the voice of Shere Khan in Disney's *The Jungle Book*. Two days before he died, Sanders checked in to a hotel near Barcelona. He left three suicide notes and took an overdose of barbiturates.

....

'That was the best ice cream soda I ever tasted.'

Lou Costello, 1906 – 1959. Lou was the funny man in the Abbot and Costello double act. The pair teamed up in 1936, performing in vaudeville and minstrel shows and soon became a successful fixture on the radio. A Broadway play followed, then a contract with Universal Studios. Although they began in supporting roles, their ability to steal scenes was such that they soon became the leads. They made 36 films and were hugely successful, with sketches like *Who's on First* becoming enduring comedy classics. During the 1950s they continued with hit radio shows and a television sitcom. The pair split in 1957 and Costello worked solo. He died of a heart attack just three days short of his 53rd birthday. His last words may have actually been 'I think I'll be more comfortable now', directed to the nurse attending his bedside, however, he had enjoyed a strawberry ice cream soda with his manager earlier in the day.

'I should have had the pickle.'

Preston Sturges, 1898 – 1959. Sturges was born in Chicago into a wealthy and well-connected family. After serving in the Army during World War I, he invented a 'kiss-proof' lipstick for his mother's company (which also produced the scarf that strangled Isadora Duncan). He followed with a string of unsuccessful inventions before turning his hand to writing stories and plays. In an attempt to make more money, he began writing screwball comedies for Hollywood where he earned a reputation for witty dialogue and strong female roles. He eagerly took the opportunity to direct his own material, delivering a number of successful movies such as *Sullivan's Travels* and *The Lady Eve*. Sturges died of a heart attack at the Algonquin Hotel in New York whilst writing his autobiography entitled *The Events Leading Up to My Death*.

....

'I can't go on.'

Freddie Prinze, 1954 – 1977. The father of actor Freddie Prinze Jr was an actor and stand-up comedian who had achieved fame on American television by the age of 19. He starred in the series *Chico and the Man* but celebrity and the long hours of work took their toll. He developed drug addictions and found relationships difficult to maintain. By 22 years of age, he already had one failed marriage behind him. He made a series of goodbye calls to his mother, his manager and his estranged wife. He told the mother of his young son, 'I love you, Kathy, I love the baby but I need to find peace. I can't go on.' Alarmed by the call, his manager rushed to Prinze's apartment. As he looked on, Prinze put the gun to his own head and pulled the trigger. He was rushed to hospital but finally died after his life support machine was switched off. His intention to commit suicide has been disputed by some of his family, despite the telephone calls and the note he left.

'That guy's got to stop... he'll see us.'

James Dean, 1931 – 1955. Although his acting career lasted only four years, James Byron Dean became one of the most iconic American actors of the 20th century. Along with Marlon Brando, he came to personify the 1950s and the emergence of disaffected, youthful rebellion. His status grew almost entirely from just three films: *Giant*, *East of Eden* and most famously, *Rebel Without a Cause*. His performances captured the brooding, disillusionment of youth and his physical beauty was suffused with an air of tragedy and complexity. Certainly, there had been deep unhappiness in his background: his mother died when he was nine years old and he was rumoured to have suffered abuse. His ambiguous sexuality only added to his appeal for youngsters unsure of themselves and their place in the world. The public and film critics alike lauded his work.

Dean was an enthusiast of fast cars and often competed in road races with his Speedster. As soon as he finished filming *Giant*, he set out to drive his new Porsche 550 Spyder to a race in Salinas, California. Just after being ticketed for exceeding the speed limit, Dean and his mechanic companion turned onto a highway known as 'the racer's road'. Driving at an estimated 85 miles per hour, Dean was unable to avoid a head-on collision with another car turning into the road. Unconscious as he was extricated from the wreck, he had suffered a broken neck and severe internal injuries. On arrival at hospital, he was pronounced dead; he was just 24 years old. His passenger survived but needed emergency surgery. The driver of the other car, Donald Turnupseed, escaped with only superficial injuries. The veracity of these last words is debatable, as his passenger was rendered unconscious by the accident and reportedly told the coroner that he could remember nothing immediately before impact. A verdict of accidental death was recorded. In a macabre twist, during the filming of *Giant*, Dean had recorded a public safety film warning of the dangers of speeding. He received two posthumous Academy Award nominations for Best Actor and his premature death seems only to have enhanced his legend, which endures to the present day.

'How were the receipts at Madison Square Garden?'

P. T. Barnum, 1810 – 1891. Sometimes, last words can sum up a dying person's fondest interests. Phineas Taylor Barnum described himself as a showman, although he was also a publisher, author and even politician. Above all, however, he was someone who made money by entertaining the American public, whether by fair means or foul. The phrase 'There's a sucker born every minute' was attributed to him (probably falsely) and he certainly profited from duping the public. He founded *P.T. Barnum's Grand Travelling Museum, Menagerie, Caravan and Hippodrome*. Dubbed 'The Greatest Show on Earth' it included a vast circus and a 'museum' where he exhibited curiosities to a gullible audience. His curios included the *Feejee Mermaid* (the upper half of a monkey sewn onto the tail of a fish). He employed a number of Native Americans as well a group of unusual looking people to be gawped at: albinos, giants and the obese. He also toured the Royal Houses of Europe with General Tom Thumb, (Charles Sherwood Stratton, who measured 64cm or 25 inches in height). Barnum suffered a stroke at his home in Bridgeport.

....

'Milan: what a beautiful place to die.'

John Carradine, 1906 – 1988. This prolific American character actor was known for roles in films such as *The Grapes of Wrath* and television series including *Fantasy Island* and *The Twilight Zone*. Towards the end of his life, he claimed to have appeared in more films than any other actor and it may be that he still holds the record. He married four times and was father to the actors David, Robert, Bruce and Keith Carradine. A fifth son, Christopher, became an architect. Just hours before his death, Carradine had ascended the 328 steps of the *Duomo* in Milan. He died in hospital of multiple organ failure, with his sons Keith and David at his side.

'Goddam the whole f*****g world and everyone in it – except you, Carlotta!'

W. C. Fields, 1880 – 1946. The notoriously irascible actor and comedian addressed these last words to his mistress, Carlotta Monti. Fields' public image was of a sharp-tongued, misanthropic drunk although some friends painted a different picture of the real man. He separated from his first wife, who was a chorus girl but continued to financially support their son. His next partner, a performer with the Ziegfeld Follies, was killed in a bar fight. Their child was fostered out but again, Fields continued to send financial help. His last partner, Carlotta Monti, was an actress and although they never married they remained together for nearly 15 years until his death. His reputation as a heavy drinker was an accurate reflection of the real man and largely responsible for his poor health in later years. He suffered from delirium tremens and died on Christmas Day (a holiday he apparently loathed) of an alcohol related stomach haemorrhage.

'Thank God. I'm tired of being the funniest person in the room.'

Del Close, 1934 – 1999. Actor, writer and ' improv' teacher Del Close was probably best known for his role as the English teacher in *Ferris Bueller's Day Off*. He died of complications due to emphysema just five days before his 65th birthday. His major legacy is the influence he had on the world of improvisational theatre. During his prolific career he taught and directed stars such as John Belushi, Bill Murray, Tina Fey, Mike Myers, Dan Ackroyd, Harold Ramis and John Candy. It was rumoured that he left his skull to the Goodman Theatre in Chicago, to appear as Yorick in their productions of *Hamlet*. However, his executor later admitted that all of his remains had been cremated and the skull she donated on his behalf had come from a medical supply shop.

'I'm tired of fighting. I guess this thing is going to get me.'

Harry Houdini, 1874 – 1926. The great showman was unable finally to escape his fate, when he died of a burst appendix. Born in Budapest, Houdini's family emigrated to the United States in the 1870s. His first stage appearance was at nine years old, performing on a trapeze. Harry and his brother Theo developed a strong interest in magic and at 17, Harry left home to pursue his dream of being a magician. He was able to escape from seemingly impregnable restraints and his fame spread beyond America to Europe, where he also toured. In the way of several magicians before and since, he began to debunk psychics and mediums, exposing the magic tricks they employed to dupe the public.

The cause of the ruptured appendix which killed him remains a matter of some debate. Popular belief is that it resulted from a punch to his stomach by a student in the audience; others believe the peritonitis had natural origins. Some assert that he was poisoned by Spiritualists.

....

'I love you.'

Oliver Hardy, 1892 – 1957. Born in Harlem, Georgia, the larger half of the Laurel and Hardy double act began his career by performing in Minstrel shows. He started appearing in films in his early twenties and first worked with Stan Laurel in 1917, although they would not pair up until some years later. He was married twice, the second time to the woman who would remain his wife until his death. Like Stan, Ollie was a heavy smoker. He survived a heart attack in 1954 and lost weight. He may also have been suffering with cancer and experienced several strokes, the last of which resulted in a coma. Ollie directed these words to his wife Lucille.

'I've had a hell of a lot of fun and I've enjoyed every minute of it.'

Errol Flynn, 1909 – 1959. Born in Hobart, Tasmania, Flynn was rebellious from an early age: expelled from every school he attended, he dabbled in a string of failed careers until he finally chanced upon acting. His handsome appearance and physical prowess soon brought him to Hollywood's attention and he rapidly rose to fame in swashbuckling extravaganzas such as *The Adventures of Robin Hood*. His off-screen behaviour hardly improved once he found stardom and controversy rarely deserted him. Renowned as a hard-drinking hell-raiser, he also faced three statutory rape charges but was cleared of them all. Flynn remained unapologetic, entitling his autobiography *My Wicked, Wicked Ways*. However, his ebullient lifestyle took its toll on his physical appearance as well as his health. He suffered liver failure and Buerger's Disease and died of a heart attack at the age of 50.

....

'I wish I was skiing.'

Stan Laurel, 1890 – 1965. Stan was born in Ulverston, England, and began his career on the British Music Hall circuit, where he was for a time Charlie Chaplin's understudy. Laurel even sailed to America on the same boat as Chaplin. He appeared in a handful of films before teaming up with Oliver Hardy in the late 1920s. Together they made numerous film comedy classics such as *Way Out West*, *Sons of the Desert* and *The Music Box*. Laurel married four wives, one of them twice, but it was rumoured that he never recovered from the death of his on screen partner, whom he nicknamed 'Babe'. After Ollie's death, Stan ceased to make any appearances in film or on stage. After suffering a heart attack, Stan was admitted to hospital. He reportedly told his nurse that he wished he was skiing. 'Oh, I didn't know you were a skier.' she answered. 'I'm not' he replied, 'but I'd rather be doing that than doing this!' He died a few moments later.

'I've got to be crazy to do this shot. I should have asked for a stunt double.'

Vic Morrow, 1929–1982. The American actor died in a freak helicopter crash during filming. Born in the Bronx, Morrow dropped out of school and joined the Navy before discovering his love of acting. Although he achieved fame in the 1960s television series *Combat!* he never quite progressed from playing 'heavies' on television and in 'B picture' movies. Subsequently, his career appeared to be on the slide until he landed a role in the big budget *Twilight Zone: The Movie*. Morrow believed this could be his professional comeback but it was not to be. In the fatal night-time scene, Morrow's character was meant to carry two Vietnamese children across a river to safety as their village was bombed. The real-life Vietnam veteran operating the helicopter lost control among the film pyrotechnics and plummeted into the water, hitting Morrow and the two child actors, killing them all instantly. Morrow was decapitated by the rotor blades, with the cameras still rolling. Judging by his half-joking last words, made just before filming of the scene began, he may have shared the safety concerns of many of the crew.

Director John Landis and four other members of the film crew stood trial for manslaughter but were acquitted. The accident prompted Hollywood to instigate tougher safety laws and CGI now makes the use of real helicopters and explosions close to live actors unnecessary.

Morrow married twice and had two children, one of whom is the actor Jennifer Jason Leigh.

'Dammit! Don't you dare ask God to help me!'

Joan Crawford, 1906 – 1977. This was the indomitable actress' response to her housekeeper who was praying over her deathbed. Crawford became a huge star in 1925 and continued to appear in classics such as *Mildred Pierce*, for which she won an Oscar. One of her greatest roles came in 1962, when she starred with Bette Davis in *Whatever Happened To Baby Jane*? The two ageing divas loathed each other: Davis once quipped that Crawford had '…slept with every male star at MGM except Lassie.' Crawford branded Davis a 'phony' but the result of their pairing on screen was spellbinding. Crawford once admitted, 'I love playing bitches. There's a lot of bitch in every woman…' and there was certainly plenty in her. She called Marilyn Monroe 'cheap', described Greta Garbo as looking like a 'bag lady', Judy Garland as '…a spoiled, indulgent, selfish brat,' and labelled Marlon Brando 'fat'.

In her later years, Crawford drank more heavily. Shocked by her appearance in a photograph in 1974, she withdrew from public life and devoted herself to vodka and Christian Science. She was divorced from three of her four husbands (including actor Douglas Fairbanks Jr.) and disinherited two of her four adopted children. One of them, Christina, countered with a devastating account of her childhood called *Mommie Dearest*, which described Crawford's capricious temper, alcoholism and cruel behaviour. Joan Crawford died of a heart attack at her New York apartment.

'Surprise me.'

Bob Hope, 1903 – 2003. This was the final gag from Hope on being asked by his wife where he wanted to be buried. Born in Eltham, England, Hope's family emigrated to the United States when he was around four years old. His show business career began on the stage, working as a dancer and comedian and his first film role came in 1938. At the beginning of the 1940s, he teamed up with Bing Crosby and Dorothy Lamour for the highly successful *Road To...* movies. With their shared work and love of golf, Hope and Bing Crosby remained friends until death. Hope achieved countless honours for his work entertaining American troops during World War II as well as the Vietnam, Korean wars.

Bob Hope was a master of the one-liner, with a razor sharp ability to deliver a gag. Ageing provided him with a rich seam of material, once remarking 'You know you're getting old when the candles cost more than the cake.' On his 80th birthday he joked 'It's the time of your life when even your birthday suit needs pressing.' At 100 he said 'I'm so old they've cancelled my blood type.'

He finally retired from show business at the age of 93 and died of pneumonia just a few weeks after his 100th birthday. He left a fortune, built partly on shrewd business sense and reputedly, a tendency towards thriftiness.

'That was a great game of golf, fellers.'

Bing Crosby, 1903 – 1977. Crosby's deep, baritone voice and relaxed 'crooning' style helped to make him one of the best-selling singers of the 20th century and a heart throb for the 'Bobby-socks' generation. His popularity as a singer during the 1930s led to the offer of film roles and he soon became one of America's most beloved actors. His song *White Christmas*, which also appeared in the hit film, *Holiday Inn* is still a seasonal fixture, as is *Little Drummer Boy*, which he recorded with David Bowie in 1977. Highlights of his long film career include the *Road to...* series of musical comedies with Bob Hope and Dorothy Lamour, *High Society* with Frank Sinatra and Grace Kelly and *Blue Skies* with Fred Astaire. He won an Oscar for his portrayal of Father O'Malley in *Going My Way*. Crosby had a weakness for racehorses but was notoriously unlucky with them: a fact which provided much comic material for his friend Bob Hope.

He was married to his first wife for 22 years until her death and they had four children together. With his second wife, a further three children were born and the couple remained married until his death. Crosby died of a heart attack just after playing golf on a course near Madrid, Spain.

SWAN SONG

Musicians and Dancers

'Leave me alone, I'm fine.'

Barry White, 1944 – 2003. So said the singer and composer, to his nurse. White survived the mean streets of East Side Los Angeles to become a major star during the 1970s, recording hits such as *Can't Get Enough of Your Love, Babe* and *You're the First, the Last, My Everything*. Affectionately nicknamed 'The Walrus of Love' by his fans, White experienced continual health problems associated with his obesity, including high blood pressure and diabetes. Finally, he suffered total renal failure and died at the Cedars-Sinai Medical Centre in Los Angeles.

....

'Okay, I won't.'

Elvis Presley, 1935 – 1977. The 'King of Rock and Roll' had just been warned by his fiancée not to fall asleep in the bathroom. His health had been in a long and steep decline caused mainly by barbiturate abuse. His girlfriend later found him collapsed on the bathroom floor and after numerous attempts to revive him failed, he was pronounced dead of heart failure.

He is buried at his home of Graceland in Memphis. The Graceland site has become a popular tourist venue, attracting around 600,000 tourists every year to see the place where Elvis lived and died.

....

'Love one another.'

George Harrison, 1943 – 2001. One-time member of The Beatles, the most successful pop group of all time, Harrison was a solo musician and film producer. He died in Los Angeles of a recurring cancer, with his family at his bedside. His beliefs in Eastern mysticism seem to have enabled him to face his death without fear and his last wish was that his ashes be scattered on the River Ganges.

'The taste of death is upon my lips...I feel something that is not of this earth.'

Wolfgang Amadeus Mozart, 1756 – 1791. The musical genius died of an unidentified fever and some intrigue surrounds his death. He is reported to have said, not long before his death, that he could not shake the notion he had been poisoned. He was working on the *Requiem* and felt that he was writing it for himself. His colleague Salieri was accused by some of having poisoned his rival but consistently denied it. Contemporary attempts at a diagnosis have indicated causes of rheumatic fever, streptococcal infection or a subdural hematoma. Mozart was buried, according to local custom, in a common grave which was later reused by the Viennese authorities, as was usual practice for the time, and so the composer's remains were lost.

....

'Money can't buy life.'

Bob Marley, 1945 – 1981. The legendary Jamaican musician died of cancer. Some years earlier, cancerous cells had been found in his toe but he refused to have it amputated because of his religious beliefs. Marley knew the end was near and tried to return to Jamaica from Europe but only reached as far as Florida before he died. An assassination attempt was made on Marley, his wife Rita and his manager during a Wailers rehearsal in 1976 but they all survived.
Marley's last words were addressed his to his son Ziggy, who was at his hospital bed. He was given a state funeral in Jamaica, where the prime minister delivered a eulogy to one of the country's best-known and best-loved exports.

'I'd like to have some more milk. Please, please give me some more.'

Michael Jackson (pictured), 1958 – 2009. Although controversy and conspiracy theories still surround the superstar's demise, much as they did his life, the official cause of death was recorded as cardiac arrest caused by drug intoxication. One of the drugs found in Jackson's system, propofol, is commonly called Milk of Amnesia and is potentially so dangerous that it is usually administered only by anesthetists for pre-surgery use. His personal physician, who was present at the death but unable to revive him, was later convicted of involuntary manslaughter. The court held that the doctor had supplied and administered the drugs which killed the singer.

Jackson's career began in childhood as part of the Jackson 5 and his solo career produced a succession of massive worldwide hits such as *Thriller* and *Billie Jean*. Following a damaging court case concerning child abuse, from which he was acquitted, Jackson had stepped back for a while from the limelight. In 2009, however, he had been about to re-emerge into the public arena with a series of live shows in London, called *This Is It*.

Jackson's death elicited such instant global interest that Twitter, Wikipedia and several other major websites crashed. Google experienced such severe strain they initially thought they were under cyber-attack. Jackson's memorial service became a show in itself, with eulogies and performances from stars such as Stevie Wonder and Lionel Richie.

'Oh, you young people act like old men. You have no fun.'

Josephine Baker, 1906 – 1975. When she uttered these words, the irrepressible Baker was apparently trying to seduce a man decades younger than her. That night, she suffered a cerebral haemorrhage from which she never regained consciousness. Freda Josephine McDonald was born into poverty in St Louis, Missouri. She first tasted success singing and dancing on Broadway but the strictures of racism prevented her achieving true success. It was only after her move to Paris in the 1920s that her star could ascend to its full height. Her dance routines were not only skilful but comedic, making her hugely popular with music hall audiences. Her willingness to appear wearing scant costumes probably did not detract from her appeal, either. Most famously, in a routine called *La Folie du Jour*, she wore only a skirt made of bananas. She rocketed to European stardom becoming one of the highest paid performers on the continent. Once again, she tried for success in her home country but was met mainly with hostility. Josephine returned to France, married a wealthy man and took French citizenship. During World War II she worked for the Red Cross, entertained the troops and even smuggled messages for the French Resistance. These efforts earned her the *Croix de Guerre* and the *Legion d'Honneur*, the only American-born woman to receive full French military honours. After the war, she adopted 12 children from different parts of the world, who she called her 'rainbow tribe'. Baker visited the United States several times during the 1950s and 1960s, lending support to the Civil Rights movement and finally, in the 1970s, she achieved acclaim in her own nation. She continued to captivate audiences in Europe until her death.

'I'm shot. I'm shot.'

or

'Help me.'

John Lennon, 1940 – 1980. Ex-Beatle Lennon was shot at the entrance to his home in New York City by Mark Chapman, an embittered and mentally unstable drifter. During an interview in the 1960s, Lennon had quipped 'I'll probably be popped off by some loony!' Chapman appears to have arrived in New York with the specific intent of killing his childhood hero. He positioned himself among the gaggle of fans that were a constant presence outside Lennon's home. When Lennon left for the studio, Chapman asked him to autograph a copy of his album *Double Fantasy*. When Lennon returned from the studio later that evening, Chapman was still waiting. He shot the musician four times and Lennon died shortly after arriving at hospital. Chapman pleaded guilty and to date, remains imprisoned for his crime.

....

'Not like this. Don't leave like this.'

Layne Staley, 1967 – 2002, was the singer songwriter with the band *Alice in Chains*. The last person known to have seen Staley alive was his former band-mate Mike Starr, who said Staley had been in a bad way but refusing medical help. The two argued and Starr angrily left the apartment as Staley called after him. The singer was believed to have died the following day, having injected himself with a 'speedball' (a heroin and cocaine cocktail). Starr later regretted that he did not seek help for his friend and blamed himself for the death. However, Staley had a long and unhappy history of drug abuse and since the death of his girlfriend had become yet more withdrawn. In an interview just a few months before, Staley had said, 'I know I'm near death' and spoken candidly of the terrible price his addiction to crack and heroin had exacted.

'This is it! Boys, I'm going! I'm going!'

Al Jolson, 1886 – 1950. Jolson was the star of the first full-length talking picture, *The Jazz Singer* and once known as 'The World's Greatest Entertainer'. He had been playing cards with friends at his hotel suite when he suffered a heart attack. Just a few weeks prior to his death, Jolson had been in Korea entertaining American troops at his own expense. The exertions of his tour of the Far East were considered a contributory factor in his death.

....

'Oinka Oinka Oinka why you awake.'

Amy Winehouse (pictured), 1983 – 2011. This was the final tweet and the last known communication from the acclaimed British singer-songwriter. Winehouse was a born rebel and a unique artist. She also had a history of drug and alcohol abuse, which seemed initially to inform much of her work, with the single *Rehab* taking her to the top of the British and American charts. However, her addictions increasingly interfered with her talent as well as her health. By the end of 2007, fans noted a decline in the quality of her performances. Over the next few years her mental state appears to have deteriorated until she had difficulty remembering her band-members' names and even her own lyrics. Her personal life also seems to have foundered, as she was divorced on grounds of adultery and often appeared publicly in a state of intoxication. It seems she managed to reign in her drug habit by 2011 and her performances and outlook improved but the alcoholic binges continued. Her bodyguard, unable to rouse her one morning, found her lifeless in bed at her home in Camden, London. With her blood alcohol level exceeding five times the legal limit for driving, the cause of death was recorded as alcoholic poisoning.

'Applaud, my friends, the comedy is finished.'
or
'Pity, pity – too late!'
or
'I shall hear in heaven.'

Ludwig van Beethoven, 1770 – 1827. The German composer of, among many other great works, the 'Moonlight Sonata' and the 'Ode to Joy'. Beethoven began to lose his hearing at around the age of 26 but continued to produce some of the most familiar and treasured music in the Western canon. His health, never particularly robust, had been failing for some time and he was bedridden by the time of his death. Friends had come to visit during a storm and one reported that his dying coincided with a terrific clap of thunder. The exact cause of death continues to attract debate. Theories include lead poisoning, Hepatitis A and alcoholism, among many others. The quotation 'Pity, pity – too late' may be the most likely of the three options. It was Beethoven's response to being sent a gift of 12 bottles of wine.

....

'Oh s**t!'

Cozy Powell, 1947 – 1988. British drummer in rock bands including Whitesnake, Rainbow and Black Sabbath, Powell was on the phone to his girlfriend whilst driving on the M4 near Bristol. His girlfriend stated that after his exclamation, she heard a loud noise and the telephone line went dead. Not only was Powell speeding along the motorway at 104 miles per hour, he was slightly over the alcohol limit and had not fastened his seat belt. When his Saab 9000 turbo blew a puncture, he crashed into the central reservation and was killed. As newspapers reported at the time, he died as he had lived: in the fast lane.

'Farewell my friends, I go to glory!'

Isadora Duncan, 1877 – 1927. The Bohemian American dancer had just departed in an open-top car, when her long silk scarf billowed out and became wound into the rear wheel of the car, strangling her. On hearing about the scarf, Gertrude Stein was reported to have said 'Affectations can be dangerous.' Isadora was a controversial figure. She was exiled from the U.S. for her communist sympathies, her appearance and way of life were considered scandalous by many of her peers but she was an important early pioneer of modern dance.

....

'My heart is crying, crying...'

Jackie Wilson, 1934 – 1984. American R&B singer songwriter of hits such as *Reet Petite* and *(Your Love Keeps Lifting Me) Higher and Higher*. The explosive physical power of his stage act influenced other performers such as Michael Jackson, James Brown and Elvis. During a 'comeback' performance in 1975, Wilson collapsed of a heart attack just as he sang the climactic lines of the song *Lonely Teardrops*. Many audience members thought it was part of the act but other performers noticed he was no longer breathing and rushed him to hospital. Although efforts at resuscitation did revive him somewhat, the damage caused by lack of oxygen was too great. He remained in a vegetative state and never uttered another word. Seven years later he finally passed away.

'Mother, I'm going to get my things and get out of this house. Father hates me and I'm never coming back.'

Marvin Gaye, 1939 – 1984. The legendary American soul singer of such classics as *I Heard it Through the Grapevine* and *What's Going On?* (which he also wrote) was shot by his father. The Reverend Marvin Gay Senior was a controlling and alcoholic minister. Marvin Jr. was advised by his management to add the 'e' to the end of his surname to avoid any unwelcome associations. Following financial difficulties and tussles with drug addiction, Gaye Jr. was forced to move back into the parental home. The gun which killed him had been taken from him by friends concerned by his talk of suicide. Marvin later gave it to his father; perhaps surreptitiously inviting him to carry out the deed. The father's difficult behaviour eventually caused Marvin to physically attack the older man. Then, as Marvin made to leave the house, he turned to address his mother and the minister fired at his chest point-blank. Although Gay Senior was initially charged with murder, he admitted to manslaughter and received five years' probation.

....

'Get my swan costume ready.'

Anna Pavlova, 1881 – 1931. The Russian ballerina, for whom the role of the Dying Swan was originally created, refused a life-saving operation on the grounds that it would have left her unable to perform. She replied 'If I can't dance then I'd rather be dead.' She died of pleurisy. In keeping with a tradition of the ballet world, her next performance went ahead but with a single spotlight marking the areas she would have appeared in. The urn containing her ashes was adorned with her ballet shoes, which were later stolen.

'I'm losing.'

Frank Sinatra, 1915 – 1998. Actor and singer Sinatra died of a second heart attack in a hospital emergency room but had also been suffering dementia. Barbara, his wife of 20 years, had been encouraging him to fight back but clearly, he knew the battle was over. Known affectionately as Ol' Blue Eyes, Sinatra was born in Hoboken, New Jersey. The son of Sicilian immigrants, he rose to fame as a 'crooner' in the 1940s and cemented his success with several film roles. During the 1960s he became politically active, campaigning for Roosevelt and Kennedy but in the following decade switched allegiances to work for Nixon and Reagan. There were persistent rumours about his relationship with the mob – particularly Sam Giancana – and their influence on his career. Sinatra married four times, the second time to actress Ava Gardner, then to actress Mia Farrow and finally to Zeppo Marx's widow, Barbara.

....

'I'm going to heaven.
I'm comin' home.'

Bo Diddley, 1928 – 2008. The legendary bluesman and rock and roll pioneer with the rectangular guitar had remained a life-long Christian. He was surrounded by family on his death bed, who sang him the gospel song, *Walk Around Heaven*. When they finished, he reportedly said 'Wow' and gave them the thumbs up before saying 'I'm going to heaven.'

Diddley was an important influence on a variety of musicians, including Buddy Holly, The Beatles, The Rolling Stones and The Clash. Just a year before his death, he suffered a stroke following a particularly energetic performance for a man nearing 80 years of age. Three months later he suffered a heart attack. Although certain that he and Chuck Berry had invented rock and roll, Diddley felt he had missed out on the financial rewards enjoyed by others who followed in their wake.

'I need help bad, man.'

Jimi Hendrix, 1942 – 1970. The unique American musician, died in a London hotel room as a result of drug misuse in circumstances which continued to be disputed, long after his death. The inquest recorded an open verdict: there was no evidence of suicide or murder. His companion, Monika Dannemann, stated that he had swallowed nine sleeping pills (many times the recommended limit) with alcohol the previous evening. Sometime during the night, Hendrix choked on his own vomit and suffocated. However, some suspicion accumulated around Dannemann, as a number of inconsistencies showed up in her story. In the 1990s, one of Hendrix's former girlfriends succeeded in having the case reopened but the investigation proved inconclusive. Dannemann killed herself in 1996.

Hendrix's musical improvisations were legendary: he could play guitar with his teeth and even behind his own back. He brought innovation to the way electric guitars were used in rock music, exploiting effects such as distortion and feedback. In 2003, *Rolling Stone* magazine named him the greatest guitarist in rock history and his influence endures to this day.

....

'If you don't like it, you can f**k off!'

Keith Moon, 1946 – 1978. The last words of notorious drummer of 1960s rock group *The Who* were addressed to his girlfriend, who had objected to his demand that she cook him breakfast. Moon subsequently overdosed on the pills prescribed to help with his alcohol withdrawal symptoms. He had a long history of alcohol abuse and was almost as renowned for his reckless and destructive lifestyle as for his drumming.

'Be inspired.'

Heavy D, 1967 – 2011. The Jamaican-born New York rapper sent this message on Twitter just before collapsing with a pulmonary embolism, probably caused by deep-vein thrombosis. Dwight Myers had earned the 'Heavy' part of his nickname with his imposing size, although his weight later see-sawed as he struggled to control it. It was believed the blood clot formed during a flight between London and Los Angeles.

....

'As this earth will suffocate me, I implore you to have my body opened so that I will not be buried alive.'

Frédéric Chopin, 1810 – 1849. The great composer left a note prompted by his fear of premature burial. His last spoken words were 'Play Mozart in memory of me – and I will hear you.'

....

'Don't worry, it's not loaded...'

Terry Kath, 1946 – 1978. The guitarist in the rock band Chicago was a keen gun collector. At the end of a party at his band-mate's house, he began to clean one of his weapons, much to his host's irritation. Kath believed his gun was safe because he had removed the magazine. However, he had seemingly forgotten that automatic weapons always house one bullet in the chamber. He put it to his head to demonstrate it was safe and when he pulled the trigger, was killed instantly. The inquest recorded a verdict of accidental death under the influence of drink and drugs. These last words have since become one of the most notorious examples of their kind from the world of rock and roll.

'There's fun in the air.'

Maurice Chevalier, 1888 – 1972. The French singer and star of films such as *Gigi* and *Can-Can* reportedly said this to the priest attending his deathbed, just before he slipped into a coma.

'I need a hospital? You're the one shot in the motherf*****g head.'

Tupac Shakur or **2Pac** (pictured), 1971 – 1996. The American rapper and actor was apparently unaware of his injuries after the car he was travelling in was attacked by a hail of gunfire. A white Cadillac, the occupants of which have still not been officially identified, pulled up alongside Tupac's car and opened fire. Initially, Tupac joked with his driver but soon lost consciousness and later died in hospital of internal bleeding. Violence was endemic among the rival rapping crews: Tupac had been shot and robbed in 1994 and was considered lucky to survive. This earlier attack had resulted in the loss of one of his testicles, gaining him the new nickname 1Pac.

'Gentlemen, I bid you farewell...'

Wallace Hartley, 1878 – 1912. Englishman Hartley was bandmaster and violinist on board the ill-fated *Titanic*. The liner sank in the North Atlantic on 15 April 1912 after striking an iceberg and Hartley reportedly led his band in playing a number of ragtime tunes. A survivor claimed to hear Hartley address these parting words to the rest of the orchestra just before they were all washed away. Newspapers of the time reported on the musicians' heroism in continuing with their duties. Hartley's body was later recovered from the sea and buried in his hometown of Colne, Lancashire.

'I'm going away tonight.'

James Brown, 1933 – 2006. The American singer, known as 'The Godfather of Soul', died of heart failure on Christmas Day, 2006. He was renowned for the high-energy showmanship of his live performances, as well as for the classic tracks he recorded such as *I Got You (I Feel Good)* and *Get Up (Sex Machine)*. He was also called 'The Hardest Working Man in Show Business' and some believe he may have worked himself to death. He continued to tour with characteristically energetic performances right into his seventies. His reluctance to complain about illness and his determination to perform, regardless of poor health, was well known among his friends and colleagues. He was finally hospitalized with the pneumonia that led to his death.

....

'Every damn fool thing you do in this life you pay for.'

Édith Piaf, 1915 – 1963. The beloved singer and French national icon, spoke these last words to her sister. Piaf died of liver cancer in 1963 and was buried at Père Lachaise Cemetery in Paris, where her grave is one of the most visited among the many famous residents. Although her reputation meant the religious authorities denied her a requiem mass, thousands of mourners lined the streets of Paris to watch the funeral procession and more than 100,000 tried to attend the burial ceremony. It was said to have been the only time since the end of World War II that the Parisian traffic was brought to a halt.

'Channel 5 is all sh*t, isn't it? Christ – the crap they put on there! It's a waste of space!'

Adam Faith, 1940 – 2003. The British singer turned actor turned manager turned financial journalist had a history of heart problems. Unfortunately, he died of a heart attack in the arms of a waitress less than half his age; something of a surprise to his grieving widow.

....

'I don't have the passion anymore and so remember, it's better to burn out than to fade away. Peace, love, empathy.'

Kurt Cobain, 1967 – 1994. The lead singer of the seminal Seattle band Nirvana left a note explaining his suicide before shooting himself in the head. Cobain was known as the 'Voice of a Generation' but always seemed uneasy with stardom and success. His family background had been dysfunctional and he had chronic health problems. Whilst these unhappy circumstances may have inspired and informed Cobain's grunge anthems (such as *Smells Like Teen Spirit*) they did little to help him through his depression and addictions. He was yet another member of 'The 27 Club': a group of musicians who died during their 27th year of life, which includes Jim Morrison, Jimi Hendrix and Janis Joplin.

THE FULL STOP

Writers, Artists and Philosophers

'I've had 18 straight whiskies. I think that's the record...'

Dylan Thomas, 1914 – 1953. Welsh poet, dramatist and legendary drinker; Dylan was born into a respectable family in Swansea, South Wales. As an adult, his reputation for drinking often outstripped his growing renown as a poet. Continual financial problems and a volatile marriage did little to temper his unruly behaviour. During his 1953 reading tour of America, Thomas fractured an arm after falling down a flight of stairs and was ejected from a performance of Arthur Miller's *The Crucible* after creating a disturbance. On his final visit to New York he began drinking heavily, despite the deterioration in his health. At a rehearsal of *Under Milk Wood* he was unable to stop vomiting and about a week before his death, a friend found him drunkenly haranguing the other guests at his hotel bar. The binges continued, punctuated by bouts of remorse, until his last day. He had been drinking continually throughout the previous day and during the evening made his notorious claim of having taken 18 straight whiskies. He awoke next morning complaining of breathing difficulties but nevertheless left his room at the Chelsea Hotel for a couple of beers. The painter Jack Heliker was at Dylan's side before he lost consciousness and reported that the poet's last words were actually 'After 39 years, this is all I've done.'

Dylan Thomas died at St Vincent's Hospital, New York and his remains were returned to his home at Laugherne. One of his most famous poems concerns death and concludes with the lines:

'Do not go gentle into that good night.
Rage, rage against the dying of the light.'

'Is it not meningitis?'

Louisa May Alcott, 1832 – 1888. The prolific author of *Little Women* was one of four sisters born in Pennsylvania to progressive and unconventional parents. Just two days after her beloved father's death, Louisa succumbed to a stroke. The underlying illness which dogged her last years is uncertain; it may have been mercury poisoning, auto-immune disease or lupus. She was buried at the Sleepy Hollow Cemetery in Concord, her grave lying across the feet of her parents' graves.

....

'No comment.'
or
'I did what I could.'

Edward Abbey, 1927 – 1989. Nicknamed Cactus Ed, this American writer had a deep love of the natural world. He also developed a strong awareness of environmental issues and worked as a seasonal park ranger during the 1960s. Through fiction and non-fiction, he explored his mistrust of industrialization and the ravages wrought on the natural world by modern civilization. His radical views on population growth and activism brought him accusations of racism and eco-terrorism; labels he vehemently denied.

His death was caused by complications following surgery. As his life ebbed away, he quipped 'No comment' to any who asked for his last words. He also gave strict instructions for his burial: rather than a coffin, he wanted his remains buried in a sleeping bag. He asked his friends to put him in the ground with the minimum of fuss and to have a party. They buried him in the Arizona desert in his old sleeping bag and toasted his life with copious amounts of whisky. On a nearby marker stone, they scratched the message 'No comment.'

'Now, now my good man: this is no time for making enemies.'

Voltaire, 1694 – 1778. This French Enlightenment writer produced poetry, novels, plays and essays as well as scientific and historical work. Voltaire became notorious throughout Europe for his attacks on the Catholic Church, his satires and libertarian values. He continually provoked the French Church and establishment, who retaliated with imprisonment and exile.

Accounts vary of his last words. Those quoted above were reported to be in response to a priest who urged him to renounce Satan. Because of his antagonism, the Church refused him a Christian burial but his friends secretly interred him at an Abbey in Champagne. Following the French Revolution, of which he was considered a key influence, the National Assembly of France had his remains moved to the Panthéon, accompanied by full honours and a procession said to have numbered a million people.

....

'Everybody has to die but I have always believed an exception would be made in my case. What now?'

William Saroyan, 1908 – 1981. This American writer made his name with ebullient and irreverent stories during the Great Depression. In 1940 he took the unusual step of refusing the prestigious Pulitzer Prize, offered for his play *The Time of Your Life*. Saroyan reasoned the play was no better than anything else he had written. He died of prostate cancer in Fresno, where he was born. Half of his ashes were buried in California and the other half in Armenia, his parental home.

'I want nothing but death.'

Jane Austen, 1775 – 1817. Austen's novels astutely observed the manners of the 18th century English middle and upper classes. Despite this seemingly distant setting, her six completed novels have become loved throughout the world, apparently more popular now than ever before. The wit and romance of her stories, along with the vitality of the characters, have endured long past her own era.

Austen was born in Hampshire, one of eight children into a creative, erudite and close-knit family. She began writing as a teenager and although her novels received some positive notices, they brought her little in the way of fame or fortune during her lifetime. It is most commonly believed she suffered from Addison's Disease but other recent diagnoses include Hodgkin's Lymphoma, tuberculosis and a variation of typhus. Despite the acute deterioration of her health, Jane continued to work for as long as she was able. She died in Winchester and was buried in Winchester Cathedral, leaving a final novel, *Sanditon*, unfinished.

'Enough already.'

William Herrick, 1915 – 2004. The American novelist who fought for the Republicans in the Spanish Civil War wrote several novels and a memoir about the conflict. He was born to Jewish parents who had emigrated from Belarus and settled in New Jersey. Highly motivated politically, Herrick had been active throughout the Depression, including attempts to organize resistance from black sharecroppers. He was quick to join the International Brigades in their fight against the Spanish dictator Franco but returned from the conflict wounded and disillusioned with the communists' methods. This disillusionment grew and by later life, he had become avowedly anti-communist. He died of congestive heart failure at his home in Old Chatham, New York.

'It's me, it's Buddy...I'm cold.'

Truman Capote (pictured), 1924 – 1984. Truman Streckfus Persons was born in New Orleans to parents who paid him little heed, preferring to farm him out to relatives in Alabama. Whilst in the care of his aunt in Monroeville, Truman struck up what would be a significant friendship with the young Harper Lee. He was later the inspiration for the character of Dill in Lee's novel *To Kill A Mockingbird*. Capote's first novella, *Other Voices, Other Rooms* established him as one of most the important writers of America's post-war generation. He followed with short stories, including *Breakfast at Tiffany's*, non-fiction (such as the innovative *In Cold Blood*), novellas, memoirs, plays and screenplays. Capote was often bullied as a youth because of his slight build and effeminate manner. However, in adulthood, his exuberant personality won him numerous friends, many of them writers, artists and celebrities. Both elite society and the Studio 54 crowd admitted him to their fold and he mingled with figures such as Jackie Kennedy, Andy Warhol and Liza Minnelli. However, after the gruelling experience of writing *In Cold Blood*, Capote's drinking escalated along with his use of tranquillizers and this inevitably affected his friendships. His long relationship with Jack Dunphy faltered as numerous attempts at drying out failed. He died in Los Angeles of liver cancer. His ashes were reportedly divided between Dunphy and another friend Joanne Carson but Carson's share were reportedly stolen and returned twice. Buddy was Truman's nickname.

....

'Well, I've had a happy life.'

William Hazlitt, 1778 – 1830. The English essayist and critic's final review was a good one. Hazlitt was also a radical and a painter, becoming England's first major critic of art and of drama. He died of an unknown illness in Soho, London and is buried there in St Anne's Churchyard.

'I feel certain I am going mad again. I feel we can't go through another of those terrible times. And I shan't recover this time... If anybody could have saved me it would have been you. Everything has gone from me but the certainty of your goodness. I can't go on spoiling your life any longer. I don't think two people could have been happier than we have been.'

Virginia Woolf, 1882 – 1941. The Bloomsbury Group writer had long struggled with mental illness and had tried before to end her life. After leaving her husband a touching letter on the mantelpiece, she drowned herself in the River Ouse, Sussex. Her body was found some weeks later, the pockets of her coat filled up with stones. Woolf's last novel, *Between the Acts*, was published posthumously.

....

'Goodnight, my darlings, I'll see you tomorrow...'

Noël Coward, 1899 – 1973. The British playwright, composer, painter, director and actor was renowned for his witticisms. However, he died during the night of a heart attack at his home in Jamaica, robbing him of the opportunity to depart with one last brilliant line. When asked about his life, he once declared that it '...really has been one long extravaganza.'

'Don't ask me how I am! I understand nothing more.'

Hans Christian Andersen, 1805 – 1875. Born into poverty in the Danish town of Odense, Andersen grew up hearing folk tales from the women in the local workhouse. His father was a poor shoemaker but owned a few books, including *The Thousand and One Nights*, which the young Andersen devoured. When he was 14 he moved to Copenhagen to work in the theatre. Although he tried his hand at acting, singing and dancing, they all came to nothing. However, a rich patron sent him to school and Hans began to write: he wrote successful travelogues, autobiographies and poetry as well as fiction for adults. His stories for children probably garnered the least attention from his contemporaries. However, when his folk tales such as *The Emperor's New Clothes* and *The Ugly Duckling* were translated into other languages, they captured the attention of foreign readers and became influential classics, with their renown spreading to the rest of the world. Andersen died of liver cancer at his home in Copenhagen. He was by then considered a national treasure and his stories such as *The Little Mermaid* are continually retold and adapted for new audiences.

....

'I can't sleep.'

J.M. Barrie, 1860 – 1937. James Matthew Barrie was the Scottish writer and dramatist who created the enduring children's classic *Peter Pan*. The boy who never grew up has appeared in countless stage and film adaptations, including a Disney version. Barrie died of pneumonia in London and is buried at his birthplace in Kirriemuir. Another important legacy of Barrie's was to bequeath the copyright of his most famous creation to the Great Ormond Street Hospital for children in London, who still benefit financially from this gesture.

'Lord help my poor soul.'

Edgar Allan Poe, 1809 – 1849. The enduring American writer, whose work so often focused on the sinister, died in circumstances which remain mysterious. He was found on the streets of Baltimore in a distressed and confused state and wearing someone else's clothes. Although he was rushed to hospital, they were unable to save him or to determine the source of his malady and he died a few days later. Poe's cause of death has continued to be a matter of conjecture. Theories include alcoholism, carbon monoxide poisoning, heart disease, rabies, syphilis and epilepsy.

....

'I am starting to believe you are not intending to count me amongst your friends.'

or

'You can take my hacienda, my land, my wealth, even – as you are going to do – my life. But there is one thing you cannot take from me: my fear!'

Pedro Muñoz Seca, 1879 – 1936. These were the last words uttered by the Spanish playwright as he faced the firing squad about to execute him. Muñoz Seca was a prolific and highly successful comic dramatist. He was also a monarchist and friend of the king. He had written plays critical of the Republic and was shot by the Republican Army during the Spanish Civil War.

'My dear, before you kiss me goodbye, fix your hair. It's a mess.'

George Kelly, 1887 – 1974. The American playwright and Pulitzer prize-winner was clearly not prepared to lower his standards, even as a female relative bent to kiss him a final farewell. George Kelly died of an unidentified illness in his hometown of Pennsylvania. Although he had been in a relationship with another man for 55 years, Kelly's family refused to acknowledge his sexual orientation. His life-long partner was even excluded from the funeral. The only family member who accepted his sexuality was his niece, the actor Grace Kelly.

....

'Take away those pillows; I shall need them no more.'

Lewis Carroll, 1832 – 1898. Real name Charles Lutwidge Dodgson, the author of *Alice in Wonderland* was born in Cheshire, England. Dodgson wrote the story to entertain a friend's daughter but it soon became extremely popular nationally and then internationally. Not long before his 66th birthday, Dodgson contracted influenza, which led to a fatal bout of pneumonia. He died and was buried in Guildford.

....

'The fog is rising...'

Emily Dickinson, 1830 – 1886. Born in Amherst, Massachusetts, Dickinson also died in Amherst, having rarely ventured away from her hometown. Only a few of her poems were published during her lifetime and she died a recluse. Following her death, her sister stumbled upon hundreds of the poems and arranged to have them published in collections. She has come to be considered one of the most innovative and influential of American poets.

'Either this wallpaper goes or I do.'

Oscar Wilde, 1854 – 1900. Perhaps it is not surprising that there is a choice of last words attributed to the brilliant Irish writer and aesthete. The 'wallpaper' quote is probably the best known and refers to the shabby décor of the hotel room in Paris in which he died. Another version has him sipping champagne on his deathbed and declaring 'Now I am *dying* beyond my means.' The formerly successful author of *The Picture of Dorian Gray* and *The Importance of being Earnest* died in ignomiy and poverty. Wilde had been shunned from polite society following a scandalous libel case in which his homosexuality became public knowledge. The case resulted in a two year prison sentence for gross indecency, which broke the writer physically, emotionally and financially.

Disappointingly, perhaps, for someone who bequeathed the world so many dazzling *bon mots*, it is likely that his final words were the incantation of prayers as his life slipped away. He died of meningitis and was initially buried outside Paris but in 1909 his remains were moved to Père Lachaise Cemetery. In 1914, the British sculptor Jacob Epstein designed a tomb for the grave but it was considered obscene and French police concealed it with a tarpaulin. A glass screen now surrounds the grave to prevent the custom of Wilde's devotees marking it with their lipstick kisses.

....

'Don't disturb my circles!'

Archimedes, c.287 – 212 BCE. The ancient Greek philosopher, scientist and mathematician remonstrated with a Roman soldier who was trying to move him on. Despite strict orders to the contrary, the soldier killed him. Among other discoveries, he is credited with inventing the catapult, the compound pulley and the hydraulic screw, and for determining the law of hydrostatics, which famously prompted him to leap from his bath crying 'Eureka!'

'Go away, I'm alright!'

H.G. Wells, 1866 – 1946. Herbert George Wells was born in Kent and became an instant success with the publication of his first novel, *The Time Machine*. A dedicated social reformer, Wells stood as a candidate for Parliament but was unsuccessful. He met Lenin, Trotsky and Stalin on trips to Russia and Franklin D. Roosevelt on a visit to America. He died of unknown causes in London and his ashes were scattered at sea. In the preface to one of his books, he claimed he wanted the line 'I told you so, you *damned* fools.' as his epitaph. Known as the Father of Science Fiction, his work is still widely read and continues to be adapted for new audiences.

....

'I am sorry to trouble you chaps. I don't know how you get along so fast with the traffic on the roads these days.'

Ian Fleming, 1908 – 1964. The creator of James Bond was born into an affluent London family and educated at Eton and Sandhurst. During World War II he worked for the Royal Navy, where he rapidly rose through the ranks. Following the war, Fleming began work on the spy novel he had long considered writing. *Casino Royale* was an instant success and James Bond quickly became a popular character. The film adaptations introduced Bond to a wider audience and continue to be a successful and lucrative franchise.

Fleming smoked and drank heavily throughout his life and he suffered a first heart attack in 1961, from which he never fully recovered. The subsequent attack in 1964 signalled the end. As the ambulance drivers rushed him to hospital, he apologized to them for the inconvenience and these were his last recorded words. Ian Fleming died the following morning and is buried at Sevenhampton, near Swindon, Wiltshire.

'If you will send for a doctor, I will see him now.'

Emily Brontë, 1818 – 1848. Although she was dying of tuberculosis, the author of *Wuthering Heights* refused to see any doctors until she knew it was already too late.

Born in Haworth in Yorkshire, Emily was the most reserved and reclusive of her gifted family. She was also stubborn and astonishingly stoic. It was said that she was once badly bitten by a dog. Despite the injury and potential threat of rabies, Emily simply walked into her kitchen and calmly cauterized the wound with a hot iron. Likewise, she preferred to die without the fuss and bother of a doctor's attentions. It is likely that the tuberculosis progressed from a cold she caught while attending the funeral of her brother Bramwell. She died surrounded by family and was buried in the churchyard at Howarth.

....

'Goodbye. If we meet...'

Mark Twain (pictured), 1835 – 1910. Samuel Langhorne Clemens was born in Florida, Missouri, and went on to write several novels under the pen name of Mark Twain. He was also a journalist, lecturer, publisher and a steamboat pilot. His witty and astute portrayal of Americana in the classic novels *The Adventures of Tom Sawyer* and *Adventures of Huckleberry Finn* helped to propel him to worldwide fame. In his later years the once cheerful Twain became embittered. He lost three of his four children as well as his beloved wife, prompting a friend to comment that his final decade was lived in hell. The man who left us with so many witty lines (such as 'Reports of my death have been greatly exaggerated.') was silenced before he could leave one last quip. He died of a heart attack in Redding, Connecticut and is buried in Elmira, New York.

'On the contrary!'

Henrik Ibsen, 1828 – 1906. The Norwegian playwright correctly asserted that he was not, as his nurse claimed, a little better. Many consider him the most significant dramatist since Shakespeare and he is often regarded as the father of modern theatre. He died in Oslo, following a number of strokes.

....

'Relax – this won't hurt a bit.'

Hunter S. Thompson, 1937 – 2005. The pioneer of 'gonzo' journalism, who wrote *Fear and Loathing in Las Vegas*, shot himself at his Colorado home. Born in Kentucky, Hunter Stockton Thompson became a journalist after leaving the US Air Force. Notorious for his drink and drug fuelled escapades, Thompson became a leading figure of American counterculture as well as its chief chronicler. It seems from his final note that he had simply had enough of life. He was bored with the restraints brought by old age and failing health. Plus, the football season had just finished.

Thompson often reminded friends that he wanted his ashes to be fired from a canon. Johnny Depp, the actor who had portrayed him in the film version of *Fear and Loathing*, paid for the canon, placed onto a tower shaped into the double-thumb gonzo fist. Six months after Thompson's death, Depp joined other friends, including Bill Murray, Jack Nicholson and Ralph Steadman at Thompson's home in Aspen for the event. As 'Spirit in the Sky' played, the canon was unveiled and fireworks containing Thompson's ashes exploded across the sky. The gathering toasted him with the chinking of ice in their whiskey glasses.

His full suicide note read:

'No more games. No more bombs. No More Walking, No More Fun. No more Swimming. 67. That is 17 years past 50. 17 more than I needed or wanted. Boring. I am always bitchy. No Fun – for anybody. 67. You are getting Greedy. Act your (old) age. Relax – This won't hurt a bit.'

'Shakespeare, I come!'

Theodore Dreiser, 1871 – 1945. Some, such as Dreiser, seemed certain of their place in the literary canon. The American novelist and journalist who wrote *An American Tragedy*, was an early practitioner of naturalism in prose. He died of heart failure in Hollywood, where he was also buried. At the funeral service, Charlie Chaplin read one of Dreiser's poems in tribute.

'What is the answer?' When she received no reply: 'Then what is the question?'

Gertrude Stein, 1874 – 1946. Stein was born in Pennsylvania but moved to Paris in 1903 where she launched her career as a writer, salon host and art collector. As a patron of the arts, she was one of the first to recognize the importance of innovators such as Henri Matisse and Pablo Picasso. Her collecting and the salon placed her at the centre of the vibrant world of art and ideas which flourished in early 20th century Paris. Aspiring and successful artists and writers found their way to her door, including Ernest Hemingway, Ezra Pound and F. Scott Fitzgerald. Some of her own more experimental writing is barely comprehensible, as she explored the avant-garde art theories of abstractionism and cubism in poetry and prose. The only commercial success she achieved was with the more conventional *The Autobiography of Alice B Toklas*. Toklas was Stein's secretary and lifelong partner and the person to whom her final words were addressed.

Gertrude Stein died of cancer in Neuilly-sur-Seine in France and is buried at Père Lachaise cemetery in Paris.

'I know not what tomorrow will bring.'

Fernando Pessoa, 1888 – 1935. The bilingual Portuguese poet, critic, publisher and philosopher wrote his last words in English. Although he was born and died in Lisbon and his identity is heavily entwined with the city, he spent part of his youth in South Africa. He wrote under a plethora of pseudonyms, each having a distinct personality and biography. He died of cirrhosis of the liver and only after his death did Pessoa gain wider acclaim for his work. His remains were later moved to the Jerónimos Monastery in Lisbon and buried alongside the graves of other Portuguese national heroes such as Vasco da Gama.

....

'Goodnight my kitten.'

Ernest Hemingway, 1899 – 1961. Winner of the Nobel and Pulitzer prizes for literature, Ernest Miller Hemingway was a giant of the American literary world. His works include *The Old Man and The Sea*, *The Sun Also Rises* and *For Whom The Bell Tolls*. He was born in suburban Illinois and worked as a journalist following service in Italy during World War I. Journalism took Hemingway and his first wife to Paris where he became a familiar figure at Gertrude Stein's salon, mixing with such notables as James Joyce and Picasso. Hemingway's personality matched the stature of his writing. Manly and hard-drinking, 'Papa', as he was known, revelled in physical challenges. He travelled widely in search of adventure, sometimes reporting on wars, other times for recreation but much of it informed and inspired his writing. He was married four times, lastly to war correspondent Mary Welsh, to whom he uttered his last words. His pursuit of physical and mental stimulation may have taken their toll in the form of liver disease, diabetes, high blood pressure and depression. On 2 July 1961 Hemingway shot himself in the head at his home in Ketchum, Idaho.

'Noli timere.'

Seamus Heaney, 1939 – 2013. The great Irish poet, winner of the Nobel Prize in Literature, texted his last words, in Latin, to his wife. The phrase means 'don't be afraid'. Heaney died suddenly in a Dublin hospital after a short illness. Heaney the poet was lauded internationally and at home, generally considered the greatest Irish poet since Yeats. Heaney the man was much loved by the general public as well as those who knew him. He was a huge public figure in Ireland but never lost his sense of shared humanity or his gentle and generous nature.

....

'I knew it. Born in a hotel room and – God damn it – died in a hotel room!'

Eugene O'Neill, 1888 – 1953. Despite success as a Nobel and Pulitzer prize-winning dramatist, O'Neill still managed to focus on the negative aspects of his life. Born in New York, he spent his early years touring the United States, accompanying his actor father. As an adult, he continued a peripatetic life, working at one thing and then another, never sticking with any job for long. Following hospitalization for tuberculosis, he began writing plays. His most important works include *The Iceman Cometh* and the autobiographical *Long Day's Journey Into Night*. Depression and alcoholism dogged him for many years but in later life he also developed a tremor which would eventually prevent him from writing. He died at the Sheraton Hotel in Boston, which later became part of the campus of Boston University. Some students claim that O'Neill haunts the room to this day. His autopsy recorded the cause of death as cerebellar cortical atrophy, a neurological disease. He is widely regarded as one of the most important American dramatists.

'Messy, isn't it?'

Richard Brautigan, 1935 – 1984. A poet, novelist and non-fiction writer, Brautigan often used black humour in his work. His suicide note was no exception, although it was perhaps darker than anything else he wrote. Brautigan was born in Tacoma, Washington and grew up in desperate poverty during the Depression and World War II. He moved to San Francisco in 1956 to pursue his dream of being a writer. He knew the beat poets but never identified himself as part of their group, despite being part of the emerging counterculture. His novel *Trout Fishing in America* brought him widespread recognition but none of his subsequent work quite lived up to its popular and critical acclaim. His star gradually faded everywhere except in Japan, where he continued to be feted. At home, however, he was devalued and forgotten and depression and alcoholism inevitably grew. He finally shot himself in the head at his California home. Brautigan planned his suicide in such a way that his body would not be found until days later, at the very earliest. He knew only too well how the decomposition of his body would produce a gruesome scene, indicated by the note left for the unfortunate who would eventually find him. The discoverer turned out to be a private investigator, possibly a month after his death. His daughter has since disputed that he left this note.

....

'I am going to the inevitable.'

Philip Larkin, 1922 – 1985. One of the pre-eminent 20th century British poets, Larkin worked for 30 years as a librarian at the University of Hull. His poetry often examined the dismal and despondent aspects of life through limpid, lyrical language. A shy and reclusive character, he declined the OBE and the post of Poet Laureate. Larkin underwent surgery for esophageal cancer but the disease had already spread too far. He is buried at Cottingham cemetery near Hull. His diaries were destroyed, in accordance with his last wishes, but the remainder of his private papers were saved.

Drink to me, drink to my health, you know I can't drink any more.

Pablo Picasso, 1881 – 1973. The prolific Spanish artist became one of the most famous figures of the art world, both widely imitated and parodied. He had a precocious talent as a child and grew into one of the most dominant forces in the art world, whose work could be recognized even by those unfamiliar with other painters. Along with Georges Braque, Picasso developed cubism, one of 20th-century art's most innovative and influential movements. Picasso's personality was equally forceful: charming and magnetic when it suited, he could also be cruel and contemptuous, with a dismal record for the treatment of the women in his life. Picasso died of a heart attack at the age of 91, after hosting a dinner party for friends at his home in Mougins, France. His widow Jacqueline never quite adjusted to his death and shot herself in 1986.

....

'LSD, 100 micrograms, intramuscular.'

Aldous Huxley, 1894 – 1963. This was the British writer's last request to his wife. He had experimented with psychedelic drugs since the 1950s and wanted to experience death under the influence of LSD. His wife obliged him as he died of laryngeal cancer in Los Angeles. His novels, such as *Brave New World,* examined and parodied contemporary society and brought him critical and popular acclaim. He also wrote essays, poetry, travelogues and film scripts. *The Doors of Perception*, in which he wrote about his experiences with psychedelics, became a cult classic for the New Age counterculture. His death was eclipsed by the assassination of President John F. Kennedy, which occurred on the same day and his ashes were interred in the family vault in England.

'So here it is at last, the expected thing.'

Henry James, 1843 – 1916. The author of *The Turn of the Screw* and *The Portrait of a Lady* was born in New York City, his father an eminent and wealthy theologian. He was educated all over Europe but finally settled in the East Sussex town of Rye. He became a British Citizen in 1915, prompted by America's reluctance to enter World War I. James' health became increasingly frail and after suffering a stroke, he died a few months later of pneumonia. His ashes were laid to rest at the Cambridge Cemetery in Massachusetts and a memorial placed at Poets' Corner in Westminster Abbey, London. His output was prolific, comprising an estimated 20 novels, 112 short stories and 12 plays, alongside travelogues, biographies and literary criticism. He once remarked, 'I've always been interested in people but I've never liked them.'

....

'Tell them I've had a wonderful life.'

Ludwig Wittgenstein, 1889 – 1951. Now generally considered one of the most important and influential of 20th century philosophers, Wittgenstein was also a mathematician and engineer. Born in Vienna, Ludwig studied at Cambridge with Bertrand Russell. His wealthy father left him a fortune but Ludwig gave all the money away. Following the publication of his only book, Ludwig concluded that he had answered all the philosophical questions, so returned to Austria to become a primary school teacher. However, he later revised this decision, returning to Cambridge University to teach philosophy. He died of prostate cancer at the home of a friend in Cambridge.

'This sucks.'

Agnieszka Osiecka, 1936 – 1997. Born in Warsaw, this daughter of a pianist father and scholar mother became one of the most eminent and widely talented of Polish citizens of the 20th century. She was not only a gifted poet but a songwriter, novelist, and dramatist among many other talents. She died following a long battle with alcoholism and colon cancer.

This was reportedly Osiecka's final comment, delivered to her family, gathered around her deathbed. She was married to Daniel Passent, a prominent Polish writer and journalist and their daughter, Agata Passent is also a journalist.

....

'Does no one understand?'

James Joyce, 1882 – 1941. James Augustine Aloysius Joyce was born in Dublin, Ireland, the eldest of 10 children. He had a prodigious intelligence, mastering 17 different languages including Norwegian, which he taught himself purely so he could read Ibsen in the original. He met and married a hotel chambermaid called Nora Barnacle and the two lived in various parts of Europe, supported mainly by Joyce's work as an English teacher. His most significant novel was *Ulysses*, the innovative work which would influence the course of 20th century literature. He suffered continual problems with his eyesight but eventually died following intestinal surgery. His death and burial were in Zurich, Switzerland.

....

'It is good.'

Immanuel Kant, 1724 – 1804. The Prussian philosopher died after a long bout of ill health which left him emaciated and blind. He was one of the pre-eminent philosophers of the Enlightenment, regarded by some as the greatest of all philosophers.

'I am about to take my last voyage, a great leap in the dark.'

Thomas Hobbes, 1588 – 1679. The 16th-century English philosopher was born in Wiltshire. During the English Civil War, he spent 11 years in exile in Paris where he taught mathematics to the future King Charles II. He died at Hardwick Hall in Derbyshire of a stroke which may have resulted from a bladder condition. Hobbes coined the familiar phrase '…nasty, brutish and short…' to describe the life of mankind in times of war.

....

'Go away! Last words are for fools who haven't said enough!'

Karl Marx, 1818 – 1883. Aware of his impending demise, Marx's housekeeper reverently asked the great political thinker for his last words. His exclamation sent her flying from the room and he was subsequently left to die in peace. Born in Germany (then Prussia), Marx spent the latter half of his life exiled in London, where he wrote his seminal work *Das Kapital*. He died of pleurisy and is buried at Highgate Cemetery in London. Below a large bust of his head, the tomb is inscribed with a quotation from his *Communist Manifesto:* 'Workers of all lands unite'.

'Only you have ever understood me – and you got it wrong.'

Georg Friedrich Hegel, 1770 – 1831. So said the German philosopher to his favourite student. The founder of dialectical thinking produced some dense and difficult work and was apparently equally perplexing in social situations. After a dinner party, the host's daughter apparently said, 'I cannot tell whether he is brilliant or mad.' Hegel died of cholera in Berlin. His sister, unable to cope with her grief, committed suicide three months later.

....

'I wish I could pass away like this.'

Vincent Van Gogh, 1853 – 1890. The great Dutch post-Impressionist painter famously struggled with his mental illnesses. His paintings now fetch record prices at auction but he died unknown and in poverty, his main support coming from his brother Theo. Vincent finally shot himself in the chest and died two days later in his brother's arms. Theo, already weakened by syphilis, was badly shaken by his brother's death and died six months later at an asylum in the Netherlands. The last line most often attributed to Van Gogh, 'The sadness will last forever' was said on his deathbed but Theo asserted that they were not his final words.

'I hope the exit is joyful and hope never to return.'

Frida Kahlo (pictured), 1907 – 1954. This was the Mexican painter's final diary entry, a few days before her death. When asked how she would like to be buried, Kahlo had asked instead for her body to be burned, saying, 'Burn it. I don't want to be buried; I have spent too much time lying down. Just burn it!' Her wishes were duly carried out and the cremation provided one last dramatic act from the Bohemian, revolutionary artist. A sudden blast of heat blew open the furnace doors and jolted her body upright. Mourners reported seeing her hair ablaze like a halo around her face and her contracting lips seemed to grin to them all, just before the doors closed again.

THE FINAL ROUND

Sports Stars, Inventors and other public figures

'I'll finally get to see Marilyn.'

Joe DiMaggio, 1914 – 1999. The American baseball star and former husband of Marilyn Monroe was born in Martinez, California, the son of Italian immigrants. He had no interest in joining the family line of fisherman but concentrated instead on his talent for baseball. His abilities brought him stardom as he brought success to his teams. During his time with the New York Yankees, they won nine World Series titles and he was elected to the Baseball Hall of Fame in 1955. Di Maggio became a symbol of the American Dream, even marrying an American icon. He and Marilyn Monroe wed in 1954, becoming one of the most high profile celebrity couples, capturing the public's imagination as well as the often intrusive interest of the international press. Although they were divorced only a year later, they remained friends until Marilyn's death. Joe never remarried but sent roses to Marilyn's grave for 20 years. He died from complications of lung cancer. On his passing, President Bill Clinton said 'Today, America lost one of the century's most beloved heroes…'

'Sleep well, my sweetheart. Please don't worry about me too much.'

Rob Hall, 1961 – 1996. The New Zealand mountain guide was trapped by a blizzard not far from the summit of Mount Everest. He had chosen to stay with a dying fellow climber, rather than use his dwindling oxygen to try and continue his descent. As a seasoned climber making his fifth ascent of Everest, he knew that rescue would come too late and used his fading radio to call his wife in New Zealand. She was also a keen mountaineer: the two had met on an attempt at Everest and he first asked her out whilst climbing Mount McKinley. The two had summited Everest together three years earlier and she would probably have been with him on this fateful attempt, had she not been pregnant with their first child.

'Just put me back on the bike.'

Tommy Simpson (1937 – 1967). Simpson was the first British road race World Champion and the first Briton ever to wear the Tour de France's coveted yellow jersey. The demanding sport of cycling has long been tainted with drug scandals and Simpson was one of many competitors who took amphetamines to improve performance. On Friday, 13 July the 1967 Tour de France competitors faced the notoriously treacherous Mont Ventoux. Temperatures had soared to 54°C, adding to the struggle to reach the 6,000 feet (1,910 metres) peak. Simpson was already suffering from dehydration and gastric problems and had drunk most of a bottle of brandy that morning in an attempt 'settle' his stomach. This combination of conditions had a fatal effect on the physically compromised Simpson; he ceased sweating and his heartbeat rose to over 200 beats per minute. Just two kilometres from the summit, he began to weave from one side of the road to the other before falling to the ground. Rather than seeking medical help, he ordered bystanders to help him back onto his bike and rode a short distance further before collapsing again. This time, Simpson had lost consciousness. He was airlifted to hospital but pronounced dead later that day without ever coming around. Many believed he had ridden himself to death. A memorial placed to him on the spot where he died has become a site of pilgrimage and the race still passes it every year. His last words, perhaps a paraphrase of his real last comments, have become cycle-racing lore, emblematic of the road cyclists' dogged determination to finish the race, no matter what. His mechanic, who had tried to persuade him to stop after the first collapse, remembered his last words being 'On...on...on...' as he rode off to his death.

'Oh God, here I go!'

Max Baer, 1909 – 1959. The American boxer who won the World Heavyweight Championship in 1934 was born in Nebraska. He was a powerful fighter who accidentally killed one of his opponents in a knockout. Baer was cleared of manslaughter but banned from boxing for a year. In 1933, Baer faced the German Max Schmeling at Yankee Stadium. Prompted by reports of the Nazi persecution of the Jews, Baer wore a Star of David embroidered onto his shorts and won the match in front of 60,000 spectators. There is some question about the extent of his Jewish heritage but the gesture made him a hero for Jewish fight fans. He was knocked out by Joe Louis in 1935 and retired from the ring in 1941 having notched up 72 victories, including 52 knockouts and only 12 defeats. Following his retirement from boxing, he continued to referee matches and appeared in a number of films and television shows. He died of heart failure at the Hollywood Roosevelt Hotel in California.

....

'One last drink, please.'

Jack Daniel, 1850 – 1911. The American distiller was born in Lynchburg, Tennessee, and named Jasper Newton Daniel. His parentage included Scottish and Irish blood, which may have accounted for his enthusiasm and aptitude for producing whiskey. The exact date of his birth is uncertain, as is the year when the distillery which still bears his name was founded but his Tennessee spirit has become the best-selling American whiskey in the world.

Daniel died in Lynchburg of sepsis. It was rumoured that the blood poisoning had been caused by an injury to his toe after he kicked a safe which he was unable to open. A popular story during his distillery tours is that he could have cured his illness had he dipped the toe in a glass of his own whiskey.

'The car seems ok...'

Ayrton Senna (1960 – 1994). The Brazilian Formula One champion was killed in the 1994 San Marino Grand Prix. Senna had previously complained about the car's handling and performance. On the morning of his death, he met with McLaren teammate Alain Prost to discuss instituting a drivers' association to improve safety standards. The day's racing had not progressed smoothly with several incidents interrupting the competition. However, Senna had regained his lead by the seventh lap, when he entered the Tamburello corner. His car suddenly left the track and hit the concrete barrier. Within two minutes of the accident, medics had pulled him from the wreck and begun emergency treatment. The champion was airlifted to hospital but declared dead two hours later. It is thought the crash was caused by a faulty steering column. His death was considered a national tragedy in Brazil and marked by three days of official mourning. Around three million people converged on his hometown of São Paulo and more than 200,000 filed past his body as he lay in state.

'My friends: my work is done. Why wait?'

George Eastman (1854 – 1932). Eastman was an innovator and philanthropist. Although in high school he was not considered particularly bright, he overcame his poor beginnings to become one of the most successful American businessmen of the 20th century. His company produced the Kodak camera and was the largest U.S. photographic company and a brand leader. He was instrumental in making photography something everyone could enjoy, rather than a specialist pastime. As his personal fortune grew, he collected fine art and donated millions of dollars to medical and educational institutions. He suffered from a hardening of the cells in his lower spinal cord which caused chronic pain and increasingly limited his mobility. Eventually, this debilitating condition caused Eastman to commit suicide and he wrote these last words in a note to his friends.

'Oh wow. Oh wow. Oh wow.'

Steve Jobs (pictured), 1955 – 2011. Steven Paul Jobs was born in San Francisco to a pair of unwed academics who put him up for adoption. His adoptive family moved to Santa Clara, which would later become known as Silicone Valley and from an early age he showed an interest in electronics as well as an entrepreneurial flair. He met Steve Wozniak (known as Woz) in 1969 when both were still teenagers and the two shared a fascination for electronics and computers. In 1972 they set up their first business venture: building and selling devices that allowed the user to make free telephone calls. The business did well but as the gadgets were illegal, the boys soon dropped it after nearly being caught by the authorities.

Steve began to dabble in Eastern mysticism and psychedelic drugs and dropped out of college. Short of money, he took a job at Atari, one of the first video game companies. Meanwhile, Woz had been working at Hewlett Packard during the beginning of the personal computer revolution and produced his own version of an early microcomputer. Steve was impressed with the results and the two went into business together for a second time: the Apple company was born. Tough and temperamental, Jobs was perhaps not always the easiest boss but his perfectionism helped to put Apple at the forefront of popular technology. In 2004 he underwent surgery for pancreatic cancer, then a liver transplant in 2009. He died at his home in Palo Alto, California due to complications caused by a relapse of his pancreatic cancer. By the time of his death, Jobs was at the vanguard of a technology revolution and his products such as the Apple Mac, iPhone and iPad had become ubiquitous in contemporary life.

'I'm going over the valley.'

Babe Ruth, 1895 – 1948. Ruth was born into a poor Baltimore family and grew into a wayward and rebellious child. His despondent parents finally packed him off to a Catholic reformatory for boys which turned the young Ruth's life around by introducing him to the sport of baseball. He was both an excellent hitter and pitcher. Ruth played for the Boston Red Sox until the club sold him to the New York Yankees. His departure ended the Red Sox's winning streak and inaugurated the start of the Yankees dominance of the World Series. Ruth set record after record during his career and was considered by many to be the greatest baseball player of all time. Babe's love of food, alcohol and women earned him a reputation for fast living. He died of cancer in 1948. Thousands of New Yorkers held vigil outside the hospital during Ruth's final days. His body was laid in state at Yankee Stadium, where 77,000 people came to pay tribute and around 75,000 gathered outside the Cathedral where his funeral service was held.

....

'Wait a second.'

Madame de Pompadour, 1721 – 1764. The mistress of the French king Louis XV made death wait a moment while she applied a dash of rouge to her cheeks. The illegitimate daughter of an exiled financier, Pompadour had been groomed from an early age to become a high-class courtesan. She preserved her status for a long period of time, employing her education as well as her beauty and intelligence to become one of the most powerful women in France. Even when his passion for her was spent, Louis retained the canny Pompadour as a close friend and political advisor. She died of tuberculosis at the age of 42, on Easter Sunday, at the Palace of Versailles. Although she was despised by the public, she exerted an immense influence on French politics and culture, including architecture, the decorative arts, fashion and literature.

'The b******s got me but they won't get everybody.'

Alexander Litvinenko (1962 – 2006). The former Russian spy made this comment in an interview just hours before he died. Litvinenko also worked for the British and Spanish secret services. He was a critic of Putin's regime and had been investigating Spanish links with the Russian Mafia. Litvinenko took asylum in Britain after claiming that a bombing blamed on Chechen terrorists had, in fact, been carried out by Russian agents as a pretext for invading Chechnya. On 1 November 2006, Litvinenko took tea with two former Russian agents at the Millennium Hotel in Central London. Soon after, he became ill and began to vomit. His condition gradually deteriorated and he was admitted to hospital three days later. On 11 November he told the BBC he had been poisoned and that he had been investigating the death of Russian journalist Anna Politkovskaya, another critic of the Russian secret service. His condition continued to worsen and he died six days later with his family at his side. The post-mortem confirmed he had been poisoned by the radioactive substance polonium-210 but Russian authorities have refused to extradite the two suspected of administering the substance. The pair deny murder, pointing instead at MI6. In his last statement, published by the *Mail on Sunday Online*, he placed the blame for his illness firmly with Vladimir Putin: 'May God forgive you for what you have done, not only to me but to beloved Russia and its people.'

....

'I am about to – or I am going to – die; either expression is correct.'

Dominique Bouhours (1628 – 1702) was a renowned French grammarian and Jesuit author. He also taught rhetoric, wrote books of criticism and translated the New Testament into French. His biographies of saints' lives were for a long time regarded as the most authoritative source. He was born and died in Paris.

'I am not in the least afraid to die.'

Charles Darwin, 1809 – 1882. The British naturalist whose theory of evolution established a new understanding of life on Earth, was born into a wealthy and eminent family in Shrewsbury and studied at Edinburgh and Cambridge Universities. During his five-year voyage on the survey ship HMS *Beagle*, Darwin began to form his revolutionary theories on the evolution of species. Although other naturalists had come close, they were unable to work out the mechanism that enabled the process of evolution. Darwin finally hit upon natural selection as the missing part of the equation. At his home in Downe, he worked for 20 years, gathering evidence and refining his theory. It was only in 1858, when he learned that his friend Alfred Russell Wallace had also hit upon the solution that he finally went public with his work. A year later, he published his landmark book, *On the Origin of Species by Means of Natural Selection*. It was an instant, albeit controversial, bestseller and his theories have stood the test of time, becoming accepted by the mainstream. He died of heart disease at Down House and is buried in Westminster Abbey, London. In his last words, he also told his beloved wife and children how good they had been to him.

....

'I'm a f*****g doctor!'

R.D. Laing, 1927 – 1989. Ronald David Laing was a controversial Scottish psychiatrist who gained fame in the 1960s and 1970s with radical 'anti-psychiatry' treatments and books such as *The Divided Self*. He believed that mental illnesses such as schizophrenia were merely a rational response to trauma, rather than medical problems to be suppressed. Laing collapsed whilst playing tennis in St Tropez. Alarmed bystanders called out for a doctor, eliciting Laing's tetchy response.

'It is beautiful over there.'

Thomas Edison (1847 – 1931). The great American inventor and entrepreneur was born into modest circumstances in Ohio. A childhood bout of scarlet fever damaged his hearing permanently and he was almost completely deaf in adulthood. Edison began by selling newspapers at the age of 12, quickly progressing to publishing his own news-sheets. He spent all of his spare time studying and experimenting, particularly with telegraphy and electrics. By the age of 22, the rights for his first invention (a Universal Stock Printer) brought him $40,000 dollars (£25,000): a huge sum for the 1860s. He continued to invent devices which brought him fame and fortune but the innovations for which he is probably best remembered are the phonograph (the first method of recording sound) and the light bulb.

He died of complications from diabetes at his home in New Jersey. At news of his passing, people around the world dimmed their lights as a mark of respect. It was unclear whether his last words referred to a vision of impending paradise or to the view just outside his window.

....

'Uh oh...'

Michael J. Smith (1945 – 1986). Smith was one of seven crew members killed on board the space shuttle *Challenger*. He was the shuttle's pilot and his was the last voice recorded by Mission Control before the spacecraft exploded. It was only 73 seconds into its flight and had reached an altitude of 48,000 feet (14.6 km). It was later revealed that the explosion was caused by the failure of the rubber O rings used on the rocket boosters. Concerns had already been raised by engineers about the O rings' performance but NASA decided to launch the mission regardless.

'KHAQQ calling Itasca. We must be on you but cannot see you. Fuel is running low. Been unable to reach you by radio. We are flying at 1,000 feet'

Amelia Earhart (1897 – 1939). This American pioneer aviatrix was born into an upper middle class family in Kansas. Her first flight was in 1920 and although it lasted only ten minutes, she was smitten. She began flying as a hobby, became the 16th woman to be awarded a pilot's license and eventually bought her own airplane. She was the first female passenger on a transatlantic flight but four years later, the shy and determined young woman became the first solo transatlantic pilot (of any gender). Earhart recorded several aviation firsts, not just for a female pilot but as the first person to fly solo in the Pacific and the first pilot to fly from Hawaii to mainland America.

Her husband ran the business side of their successful partnership, including lines in women's luggage and sports clothing as well as publishing her books on flying. It was in 1937, during her attempt to circumnavigate the equator, that Amelia and her navigator disappeared. Having already completed two thirds of the challenge, they took off from New Guinea, bound for Howland Island: a minute dot in the immense Pacific Ocean. Despite extensive land and sea rescue efforts, they were never found and their fate remains a topic of speculation. She was officially declared dead in 1939.

'I should have drunk more champagne.'

John Maynard Keynes, 1883 – 1946. This was the last wish of the influential British economist. Keynes was born into an affluent academic family. His mother was the first female mayor of Cambridge and his father an economist and philosopher. Educated at Eton, Cambridge University and King's College, Keynes proved to be a brilliant student from an early age. He fell in with the Bloomsbury Group, a set of bohemian artists and intellectuals including Virginia Woolf, E.M. Forster and Duncan Grant. Keynes worked for the treasury during the two World Wars and made himself a large fortune by playing the stock markets during the peacetime in between. He married a Russian ballerina, became a patron of the arts and was made a member of the House of Lords. Keynes died of a heart attack in 1946.

....

'Southerly gales, squalls, lee rail under water, wet bunks, hard tack, bully beef: wish you were here – instead of me!'

Richard Halliburton, 1900 – 1939. The extraordinary American adventurer and writer swam the Hellespont and the Panama Canal, rode an elephant over the Alps, dined with Haile Selassie and spent an afternoon with Madam Lenin. His final trip was in a Chinese junk with the writer Paul Mooney, with whom he was probably romantically involved. Their boat disappeared without trace, somewhere in the Pacific. There was conjecture that the Japanese may have discovered he was spying for America and killed him. More likely, it may have been that his junk was just that and the expedition sank. In his time, he was as famous as Charles Lindbergh or Amelia Earhart and his books as popular as Hemingway's and Fitzgerald's but he has since been largely forgotten.

'We got a bad fire! Let's get out – we're burning up...'

Apollo 1 astronaut (1967). The speaker was probably Roger Chaffee. He and the other two astronauts, Gus Grissom and Ed White, were all killed when fire swept through their spacecraft. They were taking part in a test run for the first manned flight to the Moon and it is thought an electrical spark ignited a fire in the oxygen tanks. Technicians took five minutes to get the pressurized doors open but the crew had probably perished within seconds.

....

'I have not told half of what I saw.'

Marco Polo (1254 – 1324). The Venetian explorer was born into a family of wealthy merchants. Polo accompanied his father and uncle on a great journey east to the magnificent summer court of Kublai Khan, known as Xanadu. For the next 17 years the Venetians explored China as envoys for the Khan. They eventually returned to Venice through Sri Lanka, India and Persia and arrived home laden with precious jewels. Marco was later captured by rival Genoese naval forces and whilst in prison recounted his adventures as a means of passing the time. One of his jail-mates was a writer from Pisa, who wrote the tales down whilst adding some imaginative flourishes of his own. The book introduced 14th-century Europeans to the 'mysterious' Eastern lands and became a European bestseller, translated into several languages. Not everyone believed his accounts, some doubting he had even reached China. As Marco lay dying at his home in Venice, visitors urged him to confess that the tales were fantasy but he firmly maintained their truth. He was buried in the Church of San Lorenzo. As time has passed, many details from his books have been supported by other sources and history has vindicated much of his account.

'Don't worry, they usually don't swim backwards.'

Steve Irwin, 1962 – 2006. The Australian naturalist and documentary film presenter apparently made this observation about a stingray he was filming on the Great Barrier Reef. However, the ray did swim backwards and the sting from its tail pierced Irwin's heart and killed him. He was an extremely popular environmentalist and presenter in Australia. In shows such as *Crocodile Hunter*, he often handled dangerous animals and occasionally his stunts provoked an outcry. Only one death by stingray attack had previously been recorded in Australia: they are not aggressive creatures and the venom in their tails is rarely lethal. It seems to have been a freak accident caused by a frightened animal. Irwin was buried at a private location in the grounds of Australia Zoo, Queensland.

....

'Utter nonsense!'

Eleanor Roosevelt, 1884 – 1962. This was the first lady's response to the nurse who told her she would die once she had fulfilled her purpose on Earth. Eleanor was renowned for her outspoken nature. When her husband, Franklin D. Roosevelt contracted polio, Eleanor became crucial to maintaining his political career. When he achieved the presidency, she gave her own press conferences and wrote a regular newspaper column; she was the first president's wife to emerge into the spotlight as a political activist in her own right. She played an important humanitarian role at the White House, speaking up for the poor and on civil rights issues. Following Franklin's death, she worked for the United Nations, mainly in the area of human rights and most particularly those concerning children's and women's issues. Eleanor eventually helped to draft the UN's Universal Declaration of Human Rights and President Kennedy appointed her chair of the Commission of the Status of Women. She died of cancer in New York and is buried alongside her husband.

'A dying man can do nothing easily.'

Benjamin Franklin (1706 – 1790). The man who adorns America's $100 bill was born in Boston, the son of a soap and candle maker. Benjamin began life as a printer's apprentice but also secretly wrote popular articles for his brother's newspaper. He finally ran away from home to escape his overbearing older brother. He eventually set up a successful printing business of his own in Philadelphia, along with a general store and a bookshop, which he ran with his wife. As his businesses thrived, Benjamin joined the Masons and contributed more to local civic improvement, including the first American subscription library, the Philosophical Society and the Pennsylvania Hospital. He also organized the city's first fire brigade and fire insurance company. Gradually, he retired from business to focus on his experiments and inventions. His contributions were prolific and diverse, including a safe, heat efficient stove, musical instruments, swimming fins and bifocals. His studies of electricity and in particular lightning brought him international acclaim. During the 1750s Franklin increasingly involved himself in politics, becoming a Colonial representative in England, where he spent several years. Gradually, he moved from considering himself a loyal Englishman to working for American independence. He helped to draft the Declaration of Independence, then travelled to France as ambassador, where his wit and knowledge made him a popular figure. In his late 1770s, he returned to America and continued in public life. One of his last deeds was to write the anti-slavery treatise of 1789. He died in Philadelphia, suffering from gout and several other ailments.

'You will not find me alive at sunrise.'

Nostradamus, 1503 – 1566.This was one prediction the French occultist apparently got right. Nostradamus began his career as a doctor, attempting to treat victims of the Plague. In 1538, he was charged with heresy and left France to escape the Inquisition. It was during his travels in exile that he was said to have had a psychic awakening which enabled him to predict the future. His visions were published in a set of almanacs and his long-term predictions collected in a book called *Les Prophesies.* His books were extremely popular although some thought his prophesies came from the Devil, some that he was insane, whilst others simply considered him a charlatan. His predictions were recorded in ambiguous language which could be later interpreted to fit almost any event. However, his services as a fortune-teller and astrologer were sought by European royalty and elite families such as the Medici. Gout and arthritis plagued his adult life and the condition eventually developed into dropsy which brought about a heart attack. Nostradamus reportedly predicted he would not survive the night and they duly found him dead in his room the next morning.

....

'In keeping with Channel 40's policy of bringing you the latest in blood and guts and in living colour, you are going to see another first – attempted suicide.'

Christine Chubbuck, 1944 – 1974. The American morning-show host announced her suicide live on her television show, drew a revolver from her bag and shot herself in the head. The studio cameras cut to black, then broadcast a public service film but hundreds of viewers had seen the presenter kill herself.

'I am just going outside. I may be some time.'

Captain Lawrence Oates (1880 – 1912). Oates was employed by Captain Scott to care for the ponies on the British expedition to the South Pole. The decision to use ponies in the Antarctic was just one of several fatal mistakes the British party made. They reached the South Pole only to find that the Norwegian flag had already been planted there by Roald Amundsen. As the British expedition turned back, the sub-zero temperatures and hostile weather conditions gradually worsened and began taking their toll. Petty Officer Evans was the first to die. Oates struggled on with frostbitten feet until he could go no further. He wanted to avoid impeding the group but his request to stay behind at a depot would have meant his certain death and was refused.

Oates struggled on a little longer but knew his failing physical health was endangering the expedition. Whilst the group sheltered from a blizzard, Oates stumbled out of the tent into -40°c temperatures, telling Captain Scott he was 'just going outside'. His death and last words were recorded in Scott's journal which was found later. They became renowned as an example of self-sacrifice but his deed was in vain. A punishing blizzard prevented the three remaining men from reaching the next depot and they also perished. Their frozen bodies were recovered just 11 miles (18km) short of the food store. Captain Oates› body has never been found.

'Beautiful'

Dr Timothy Leary, 1920 – 1996. The American writer, psychologist and advocate of LSD and 1960s counter-culture, was the originator of the phrase, 'Turn on, tune in, drop out.' A Harvard psychology professor, Leary experimented with hallucinogenics, claiming he learned more during his first 'trip' than in 15 years of study and research. Harvard eventually sacked him: not only did he fail to attend classes but admitted giving LSD, which was legal at the time, to hundreds of students. Leary advocated psychedelics in the treatment of several conditions including alcoholism and the rehabilitation of prisoners. However, his high profile antics contributed to the drugs' widespread prohibition. Some current medical research has suggested that psychedelics may indeed be valuable in treating a number of disorders. During his later years, he turned to the study of virtual reality and cyber culture.

Timothy Leary died from prostate cancer. At his request, his death was videotaped. He repeated the phrase 'Why not?' during his last moments ending with 'Beautiful.' A portion of his ashes was placed into a capsule (along with ashes from Gene Rodenberry, creator of *Star Trek*) and launched into orbit around the Earth.

....

'Just a lot of damnfoolery!'

Oliver Wendell Holmes, Jr., 1841 – 1935. This was the final judgement of Holmes, the Supreme Court Justice, as he surveyed the extensive medical equipment surrounding his bed. Known as the Great Dissenter, he was the son of eminent writer and physician Oliver Wendell Holmes, Sr. and the abolitionist Amelia Lee Jackson. Holmes Jr. fought for the Union and was wounded in the American Civil War before returning to study law at Harvard. He rose to the very highest judicial posts in America and was instrumental in shaping contemporary American law. He finally retired from the Supreme Court at 90 years of age and died of pneumonia in Washington, D.C. He was buried at the Arlington National Cemetery.

'Am I dying or is it my birthday?'

Nancy Astor (1879 – 1964). On awaking to see friends and family gathered around her bed, Nancy gave one last example of her famous wit. Born in Virginia in the United States, the Anglophile Nancy Langhorne moved to England following a disastrous marriage. Outspoken, funny and flirtatious, Nancy acquired many eligible suitors but settled on the extremely wealthy Waldorf Astor. Waldorf had been the Member of Parliament for Sutton but when he inherited a seat in the House of Lords, Nancy became the new Conservative candidate. Employing her considerable charm and wit, she won the election in 1919, becoming the first woman to take a seat in the House. (Another woman had previously been elected but as a member of Sinn Fein had refused to take the oath and so never attended Parliament.) In the face of openly misogynistic behaviour from the all-boys club of the Houses of Parliament, she campaigned for temperance and on women's and children's issues. Nancy's reputation was tainted by her anti-Catholicism and racism and in particular her anti-Semitism. Although she was not wholly in favour of the Nazis she supported appeasement to avoid another war. She was also a vehement opponent of Communism and on a trip to Soviet Russia (accompanying her friend George Bernard Shaw) Nancy openly criticized Stalin to his face. At the 1945 general election, Waldorf and the Conservative party persuaded Nancy she would not be re-elected, pressing her to stand down instead. Reluctantly and resentfully she did so. Nancy died at her daughter's home in Lincolnshire, having become increasingly isolated.

'I'll sleep well tonight.'

Henry Ford, 1863 – 1947. The inventor of the Model T Ford motor car was raised on a farm in Michigan and showed an early aptitude for technology. When his father gave him a pocket watch for his 15th birthday, Ford promptly took it apart and reassembled it – and it apparently continued to work. His sights were set beyond the family farm and so he left for Detroit, where he took employment as a machinist and studied bookkeeping. He later joined the Edison Illuminating Company, where he was promoted to chief engineer. He showed his first plans for a motor car to Edison, who encouraged him to develop them further. In 1903, he established the Ford Motor Company and in 1908, the Model T Ford. Using production lines of skilled workers, he was able to mass produce vehicles which were affordable to the general population: half of all the cars in the United States in 1918 were said to be Model Ts. Although he was a philanthropist and a committed pacifist, he was also an anti-Semite. Ford died of a brain haemorrhage at his Dearborn estate in Michigan.

....

'Leave the shower curtain on the inside of the tub.'

Conrad Hilton, 1887 – 1979. When asked whether he had any final words of wisdom, this was the Hotel chain owner's reply.

Hilton bought his first hotel in Texas in 1919 and continued to add more properties, although the Great Depression had nearly bankrupted him. Every hotel in his empire had its own identity and the chain became the largest hotel company in the world. He married three times, including the actress Zsa Zsa Gabor, and had three sons and a daughter. One of his sons took on the family business when his father retired. Hilton died in hospital in Santa Monica, California at the age of 91.

'I'd hate to die twice, it's so boring.'

Richard Feynman (1918 – 1988). The brilliant American Nobel prize-winning physicist helped develop the atomic bomb, translated Mayan hieroglyphs and was instrumental in solving the riddle of why the *Challenger* space shuttle exploded. He was also a passionate bongo player and expert safecracker. His curiosity about the world around him was the catalyst for much of his groundbreaking work in quantum electrodynamics, superfluidity and other esoteric fields of physics. Feynman was born in New York City and studied at M.I.T. and Princeton University. He went on to teach physics at Princeton, Cornell and the California Institute of Technology (Caltech). His Caltech lectures were collected into three volumes, *The Feynman Lectures on Physics*, which continue to be key texts for students and professors alike. Some lectures were filmed and have become YouTube favourites, along with fascinating interviews in which he explains concepts such as the science encompassed in a simple flower. His playful nature and talent for storytelling still help to communicate complex ideas to a mass audience.

He married three times. His first wife died of tuberculosis, the second marriage ended shortly but the third lasted until his death, producing one son and an adopted daughter. Richard developed two rare forms of cancer, one after the other, which eventually prevented him from continuing with the work he so loved. Dialysis could have prolonged his life for a few more months but because he was so debilitated, he decided against it.

'I wish I had time for one more bowl of chilli.'

'Kit' Carson, 1809 – 1868. The American frontiersman Christopher Houston 'Kit' Carson was born in Madison County, Kentucky on Christmas Eve. The family moved to Missouri and following the death of his father, Kit abandoned his schooling to help on the family farm. He would remain embarrassed about his illiteracy for the rest of his life. At the age of 14 he left home and headed west, supporting himself with labouring jobs while he acquired the skills necessary to become a trapper. He learned from and then became one of the most celebrated of the 'mountain men'. Carson was later employed as a guide for expeditions into the Rocky Mountains, California and the Pacific Northwest among others. His ability to survive in the wilderness brought him recognition as a popular folk hero and his character began appearing in Western pulp fiction. Kit later worked with the Native Americans in New Mexico and had considerable sympathy for their plight, although he fought against particular tribes during the Civil War and repeatedly battled the Navajo. He died of a ruptured aneurism at his home in Colorado, by which time he had become a symbol of the American West. Another version of his last words is 'Doctor, compadre, adios!'

'This is a sharp medicine but a sure remedy for all evils.'

Sir Walter Raleigh (c.1552 – 1618). The favourite courtier of Queen Elizabeth I of England was beheaded for treason by her successor, James I. Raleigh was a talented soldier, explorer and writer, although most of his writings were destroyed after his death. Following service in Ireland, where his brutality was notorious, Raleigh established the Roanoke colony in the New World. He explored the American coast from North Carolina down to Florida and christened the region Virginia in honour of the Virgin Queen. He made many attacks on Spanish ships, earning himself the reputation in some quarters as a pirate but bringing lavish treasures back to England, which pleased the monarch. Perhaps most famously, he introduced tobacco and potatoes to England and Ireland. Raleigh invoked the queen's displeasure when she learned he had secretly married one of her handmaids and he was promptly flung in the Tower of London for a spell. Under James I's orders, he searched for gold in South America but returned empty handed. King James distrusted him and eventually had him beheaded at Westminster. The last words were supposedly said as he eyed the axe. In another version, he was reported to have urged the executioner, 'Strike, man, strike!' His head was embalmed and presented to his wife.

VIVA!

Royalty, Religious and Political Leaders

'I live!'

Caligula, 12 – 41 AD. The third of Rome's emperors and one of the most notorious, history portrays Caligula as a mad, cruel tyrant but it is hard now to be certain just how much of this reputation was shaped by the enemies who outlived him. His real name was Gaius Julius Caesar Augustus Germanicus; Caligula was a childhood nickname meaning 'little boots'. As the great grandson of the exalted Augustus Caesar, he was an extremely popular leader among the ordinary people of Rome. He encouraged this adulation by spending huge amounts of money on public entertainments and abolishing sales tax. However, as he courted popularity among ordinary Romans, he made enemies among the ruling elite with high-handed behaviour such as an insistence on being treated as divine. He is rumoured to have committed incest with his sisters and to have threatened to make his horse a senator. After only four years as emperor, Gaius was assassinated in his palace by the Praetorian Guard, along with his wife and daughter. He was reportedly stabbed 30 times in a plot which probably involved the Senate.

....

'You must pardon me, gentlemen, for being the most unconscionable time a-dying.'

King Charles II, 1630 – 1685. This British monarch, who probably died of kidney disease, has two sets of last words attributed to him. One concerns his mistress, the actress of humble origins, Nell Gwynne: 'Let not poor Nelly starve.' His father, Charles I, had been executed following the Civil War and Charles II's reign saw the restoration of the British monarchy and included the Plague and the Great Fire of London in 1666. Although he claimed to have at least 14 illegitimate children, his marriage had produced no heir, so he was succeeded by his brother James.

'What an artist the world is losing in me.'

Nero, 37 – 68 AD. The notorious Roman emperor was accused of much eccentric and abhorrent behaviour. He considered himself a great poet and actor and even performed in public: behaviour deemed unseemly for an emperor. His story is littered with corpses. To expedite Nero's path to becoming emperor, his mother Agrippina may have poisoned his adoptive father, Claudius. Some years later, Nero apparently ordered Agrippina's murder. He was also rumoured to have poisoned his own advisor and kicked his pregnant wife Poppaea to death. Perhaps the most famous image of Nero is of the mad emperor, fiddling while Rome burns. Many did think him culpable for the great fire but Nero directed blame at the Christians, who were at the time an obscure religious sect. As opposition built against him, Nero was forced to flee Rome. When the Senate declared him a public enemy and sentenced him to death, he committed suicide with the help of his secretary.

....

'I will see you tomorrow, if God wills it.'

Pope John Paul I, 1912 – 1978. Cardinal Albino Luciani became Pope just 33 days before his death, making his one of the shortest Papacies in history. On the morning of 26 August he was found dead, sitting up in bed, still wearing his spectacles and clasping some papers in one hand. The authorities announced he had suffered a heart attack the night before. Some inconsistencies from the Vatican have led to conspiracy theories concerning the death. These suggest the Pope was murdered to prevent him uncovering Mafia-related financial scandals.

'I'm so bored with it all.'

Winston Churchill (pictured), 1874 – 1965. The British World War II prime minister was born at Blenheim Palace, the son of an aristocratic Tory politician. Winston studied at Harrow and Sandhurst before joining the Army and fighting in India and the Sudan. During the Boer War, he also worked as a journalist and made headlines himself after escaping enemy capture. In 1900, he was elected a Conservative Member of Parliament but became disillusioned with the Tories and transferred to the Liberal party. During World War I, Churchill saw active service at the Western Front as well as serving in Government. Following the conflict, he became a deeply unpopular figure by opposing Indian self-rule and supporting Edward VIII during the abdication crisis. Churchill also warned a largely indifferent public about the rise of Nazism in Germany. His insistence that Britain should re-arm fell mainly on deaf ears but he was vindicated in 1939 when war broke out between the two countries. With Chamberlain's resignation, Churchill stepped into the role of prime minister. His wartime leadership was characterized by a steadfast refusal to surrender, which helped to galvanize the British people against their foe. Despite his wartime efforts, he lost the Premiership in the 1945 General Election, regaining it in 1951 until he resigned in 1955. Depressive and alcoholic, Churchill's health had been precarious since at least 1941, when he had suffered a heart attack during a visit to the White House. Another heart attack followed a couple of years later along with a bout of pneumonia and several strokes, all of which remained secret whilst he retained political office. Finally, at the age of 90, he suffered a severe, incapacitating stroke and nine days later he died at his home in London. Britain honoured him with a week's mourning and a state funeral. Churchill was a skilled painter, often taking comfort in art. As well as history, biography and autobiography, he wrote a novel and was awarded the Nobel Prize for Literature. His writings and speeches have continued to inspire leaders to the present day.

'Pardon me, sir. I did not do it on purpose.'

Marie Antoinette, 1755 – 1793. Ever mindful of good manners, even on her way to the guillotine, Marie Antoinette apologized for accidentally treading on her executioner's foot. The Austrian born Antoinette wed Louis XVI, King of France; the two married to cement an uneasy alliance between their two countries. The young Marie found it difficult to adjust to life at the French Court. When she was just 19 years old, her husband was crowned king and she became the last queen of France. Whilst Louis was reserved, diligent and quiet, Marie was an extrovert who loved extravagant parties and elaborate fashions. She began to spend more time away from the king, fuelling rumours of an affair. As France slid into financial crisis and political turmoil, Marie's lavish spending became more conspicuous but the growing public criticism failed to curb her lifestyle. On 14th July 1789 the storming of the Bastille inaugurated the French Revolution. However, it was not until September 1792 that the monarchy was officially abolished and the king and queen arrested. Louis was tried by the Republic for treason and executed by guillotine in January 1793. The following October, Marie was also tried for treason as well as theft and sexual abuse. She was found guilty on all counts and sentenced to death. Her most famous quotation, 'Let them eat cake', concerning the starving population's lack of bread was almost certainly apocryphal but it does indicate how she was viewed by the French public.

'Oh, yes; it is the glorious Fourth of July. It is a great day. It is a good day. God bless it. God bless you all.'

John Adams, 1735 – 1826. As he lay dying, the second president of the USA was asked if he knew what day it was. Adams was a descendent of one of the English Puritans who first colonized Massachusetts Bay; he studied law at Harvard and helped to draft the Declaration of Independence. Adams narrowly missed out on a second Presidential term to Thomas Jefferson but the two men later rekindled their friendship. They corresponded with each other until the end of their lives, which coincidentally occurred on the exact same day: the 4th of July. Another, perhaps more likely version of his last words is: 'Thomas Jefferson survives' but Jefferson had died a few hours earlier. Adams' son John Quincy Adams became the sixth president of the United States.

....

'This is the last of Earth! I am content!'

John Quincy Adams, 1767 – 1848. Before he became the sixth president of the USA, Adams Jr – the eldest son of John Adams – had been a successful diplomat, having accompanied his father on his diplomatic missions in Europe. Also like his father, he studied law at Harvard. After losing the Presidency, Adams won a seat in the House of Representatives where he continued his efforts against slavery. Whilst arguing in the House of Representatives for veterans of the Mexican War to be honoured, Quincy Adams collapsed from a stroke. He died two days later in the Speaker's Room at the Capitol Building and was buried alongside his parents at the First Parish Church in Quincy, Massachusetts.

'Amen.'

Pope John Paul II, 1920 – 2005. Born in Wadowice, Poland, Cardinal Karol Józef Wojtyla became the first non-Italian pope for more than 400 years. He was elected leader of the Catholic Church in 1978 and spent much of his reign travelling the world. His relative youthfulness and charisma at the beginning of his papacy helped to make him extremely popular among ordinary Catholics. In 1981, however, an attempt was made on his life when he was shot twice whilst in St Peter's Square in Rome. He recovered from his wounds and forgave the attacker. In later years he visibly deteriorated and one of his doctors revealed he was suffering from Parkinson's disease. He died at his Vatican residence and more than three million people filed past his coffin while he lay in state. In 2013 the Vatican announced that John Paul II would become a saint, a record time for beatification.

'To the strongest!'

Alexander the Great, 356 – 323 BCE. As Alexander's life ebbed away, his advisors asked who his vast kingdom should pass to and this was his reply. By the time of his death, at only 33 years old, Alexander III of Macedon had become king of a vast area. His realm included all of Greece and reached north to the Danube, south into Egypt and eastward into Syria, Iraq and even as far as the Indian Punjab. He was a brilliant and daring general who commanded extraordinary loyalty from his men, although he could be ruthless if opposed. His army conquered the formidable Persian Empire without a single defeat and this cultivated Alexander's increasing belief in his own divinity. He died in Babylon after a ten day fever which some claimed was the result of poison but may have been malaria. No one else could rule such an immense empire and it began to fragment as soon as he died.

'The machinery is worn out.'

Woodrow Wilson, 1856 – 1924. The 28th president of the United States of America took a pragmatic view of his condition after suffering a stroke in 1924.

....

'I have tried so hard to do right.'

Grover Cleveland, 1837 – 1908. The 22nd and 24th president of the United States of America was born in Caldwell, New Jersey, the son of a Presbyterian minister. Grover bought his way out of military service during the Civil War and studied Law, becoming a district attorney. He worked his way up to becoming Governor of New York, where his physical size earned him the nickname Uncle Jumbo. Cleveland was elected president in 1885 and married a much younger woman whilst in office, still the only 'White House Wedding' in history. He had a second term of office between 1893 –97. Cleveland opposed women's suffrage as well as subsidies and special interests, believing that adversity built character. He died of a heart attack at his home in Princeton with his wife at his bedside.

'All my possessions for a moment of time.'

Elizabeth I, Queen of England (pictured), 1533 – 1603. The last of the Tudor monarchs ruled for 45 years in dangerous and demanding times, later regarded as a Golden Age. When she was two years old, her father had her mother beheaded but another wife of Henry VIII took the young Elizabeth under her wing and ensured she was fully educated. Following her Catholic half-sister Mary's death in 1558, Elizabeth became queen. A perceptive and intelligent woman, fluent in six languages, Elizabeth would need all of her considerable resources to navigate the perilous waters of state. She returned England to the Protestant faith instigated by her father and shrewdly surrounded herself with dependable advisors in a time rife with political intrigue and double agents. During her reign, England flourished in international trade, the arts and discoveries, avoiding many of the threats from abroad and within. Elizabeth never wed, insisting that she was married to her country. Against all the odds, she died of natural causes at Richmond Palace, aged 70 and she is buried at Westminster Abbey.

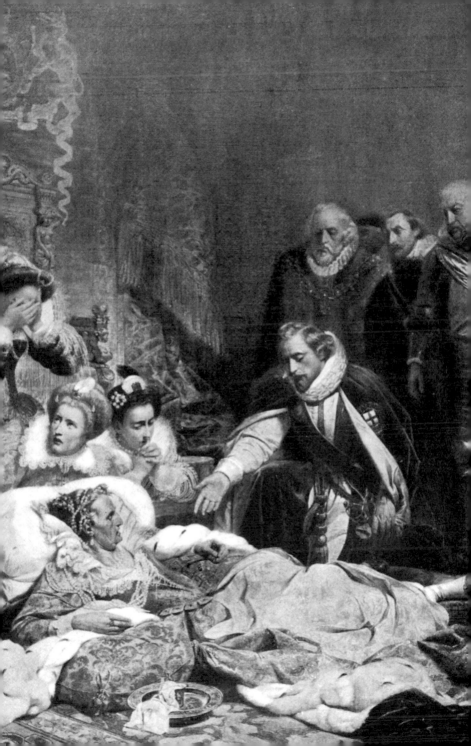

'So here it is!'

Cleopatra, c.69 – 30 BCE. Although shrouded in myth, the real Cleopatra VII was the last of the Ptolemaic dynasty of pharaohs who ruled Egypt for many generations. She was a skilful linguist and the first of the Ptolemies (descendants of a Greek general) to speak Egyptian. According to Roman historians, her appeal lay in her intelligent and entertaining conversation as well as the magnetic force of her personality, rather than her physical appearance. Cleopatra was a shrewd ruler who increased the size of her kingdom in difficult circumstances. For many years she successfully negotiated Egypt's independence from Imperial Rome: she had a son with Julius Caesar and two with Mark Anthony. Finally, she was forced into siding with Anthony against Octavian and this turned out to be the losing side. When Octavian took Alexandria, Cleopatra took her own life. The enduring, romantic version of her death is that she took an asp to her breast and used its poisonous bite to kill herself. In truth, her method of despatch is not known (or her final words, for that matter). She may have used a more dependable, pain-free cocktail of hemlock, opium and aconite, possibly administered by needle. However, it does seem likely that she preferred to take her own life rather than submit to the humiliation of defeat.

'Woe. I think I'm becoming a god.'

Vespasian, 9 – 79 AD. According to the historian Suetonius, this emperor was renowned for his sense of humour, even in the face of great peril. Roman emperors were often deified after their death, so it appears Vespasian was joking even in the face of his own demise. He died after a fever and severe diarrhea. Vespasian donated many public buildings to Rome, perhaps most famously the Colosseum, the construction of which was completed in AD 80 by his son Titus.

'Oh my country! How I leave my country!'

William Pitt the Younger, 1759 – 1806. Twice prime minister of Britain, Pitt was the son of an eminent statesman, the Earl of Chatham (Pitt the Elder). The younger Pitt was precocious, graduating Cambridge University at 17 years old and elected to Parliament at the age of 21. King George III asked Pitt to form a government after dismissing the previous coalition. So, at 24 years old, Pitt became the youngest ever prime minister of Britain. Despite being almost immediately defeated in Parliament, he refused to resign and won the next general election. Although he moved against an Irish rebellion, he also attempted to abolish the restrictions there against Catholicism. The King's staunch opposition to Catholic equality forced Pitt's resignation. However, because of the threat emanating from Napoleon's forces, George III had to ask Pitt to form another government and he became prime minister for a second time. Pitt had been sickly since childhood and his health deteriorated as the national woes took their toll. In addition, he was a heavy drinker, particularly of port, which did nothing to improve his gout. Pitt probably died of a peptic ulcer, deeply in debt and was buried in Westminster Abbey. Another version of his epitaph is 'Oh my country! How I love my country!' and yet another, more prosaic version is 'I think I could eat one of Bellamy's veal pies.'

'Don't worry, relax!'

Rajiv Gandhi, 1944 – 1991. The son of Indira Gandhi was prime minister of India from 1984-1989. His leadership was continually tainted by scandal and he lost the following election. Whilst campaigning in South India he was blown apart, along with 14 bystanders, by a female suicide bomber believed to be a Tamil Tiger.

'Cool it, brothers.'

Malcolm X (pictured), 1925 – 1965. Malcolm Little was born in Omaha, Nebraska, the son of a preacher and early civil rights worker. His father's activism brought unwelcome attention from white supremacist groups such as the Ku Klux Klan. When the family's home was burned down by a racist mob, the all-white emergency services refused to act; instead the firemen and police stood and watched as the house was destroyed. Malcolm's father was found dead two years later, probably murdered by racists but officially declared a suicide. Although he excelled at school, Malcolm dropped out at 15 and fell into bad company and criminal activity. Inevitably, he found himself in jail, where he read widely. Whilst in prison, he converted to Nation of Islam and discarded his 'slave name' for the surname X. With his intelligence and gift for oratory, he rose through the ranks of the Nation of Islam organization, bringing in hundreds, even thousands of new recruits. His promotion of 'any means necessary' in the struggle won him supporters as well as critics, including Dr Martin Luther King, who advocated peaceful means and integration. Despite his success, Malcolm became disillusioned and left the movement. He travelled to Mecca and made the Hajj, where he experienced a revelation against violent action and for global brotherhood. On 21 February 1965 Malcolm was just about to deliver a speech when three gunmen shot him dead at point blank range. All three assassins were members of the Nation of Islam. His *Autobiography of Malcolm X* helped to enshrine him as one of the most important activists of the 20th century.

'B****r Bognor!'

King George V, 1865 – 1936. This royal epitaph is almost certainly apocryphal but lives on in the popular imagination. As the story goes, the monarch was not in the best of tempers when it was suggested he return to Bognor for another curative stay. Prince George had enjoyed a career in the Navy until the death of his elder brother made him next in line to the British throne. He became king in 1910 and won respect from many of his subjects by visiting troops on the front line during World War I. The anti-German sentiment which became rife in Britain because of the war prompted George to change his family name from Saxe-Coburg-Gotha to Windsor, the name the present Royal family still carry. Long of ill health and a heavy smoker, he finally died of a chest infection at the Royal Estate of Sandringham in Norfolk. His doctor reported his last words as 'God damn you!' directed at a nurse who had just administered him a sedative.

....

'It is nothing...it is nothing.'

Franz Ferdinand, Archduke of Austria-Hungary, 1863 – 1914. Ferdinand's assassination in Sarajevo was instrumental in triggering the events leading to the outbreak of World War I. In the second attempt on his life that day, the heir to the Austro-Hungarian Empire was shot by a Serbian terrorist group. Before lunch, The Black Hand gang had attempted to blow up his car using grenades. However, they missed his vehicle and hit the one behind, injuring some of the Archduke's attendants. After lunch, Ferdinand wanted to visit the injured in hospital but his driver took a wrong turn and as he tried to reverse another terrorist emerged and shot first the duchess, who was killed instantly and then Ferdinand, who died soon after in hospital. He apparently repeated the phrase 'It is nothing' several times before he died. Gavrillo Princip, who fired the fatal shots, was too young to be executed, so was sentenced instead to 20 years in jail but contracted tuberculosis and died in prison four years later.

'We committed an act of revolutionary suicide protesting the conditions of an inhumane world.'

Reverend Jim Jones, 1931 – 1978. These were the last recorded words of the founder of the People's Temple. Around 900 members of his cult committed a mass-suicide at their compound in Guyana, known as Jonestown, in 1978. The death toll included 276 children.

Jones began preaching in a Methodist church in Indianapolis and earned a reputation as an inspirational healer. He formed his own church and began broadcasting sermons on local radio. As his congregation grew, he moved them to northern California and spread his evangelical message further afield. Although he discouraged his followers from forming sexual relationships, he indulged himself in several adulteries. The increasingly paranoid Jones moved his church once again, this time to Guyana, accompanied by around 1,000 of his followers. The People's Temple was run like a prison camp with beatings, strict food rations and armed guards preventing escape. Jones also began training his congregation in suicide drills. A California congressman, accompanied by reporters, visited the compound to investigate claims of imprisonment. They spent three days at the camp but were shot by Jones' henchmen as they tried to leave from the local airstrip. This crisis triggered the enactment of Jones' 'revolutionary suicide'. A lethal drink consisting of cyanide and Valium mixed into grape-flavour Flavor Aid (not the Kool-Aid of popular lore) was administered to all, except Jones who died of gunshot wounds to the head.

'Eva is leaving.'

Eva Perón, 1919 – 1952. Known as Evita, the First Lady and 'Spiritual Leader' of Argentina was born poor and illegitimate but dreamed of becoming a famous actress. The charming and attractive young woman quickly achieved stage and radio success in Buenos Aires but her true starring role began when her husband, Juan Perón, became president in 1946. With her theatrical background, she was a talented public speaker and used her position to fight for issues close to her heart. Evita publicly campaigned for causes such as women's suffrage and helping the poor, winning the adoration of ordinary people. Unofficially, she directed the health and labour ministries. She turned down the position of vice president, possibly due to the army's opposition or to her failing health. When her husband won the presidency a second time, she made her final public appearance. A month later, at only 33 years of age, Evita died of cervical cancer, sparking a period of passionate public mourning. Her remains were embalmed with the intention of keeping them on show. However, following Perón's overthrow in a military coup three years later, the opposition removed her body and hid it in a crypt in Milan. It was discovered in 1971 and sent to Perón, who had re-married and was exiled in Spain. The couple kept the body in their living room and his new wife arranged Eva's hair every day. When the Peróns returned to power in Argentina, Eva went with them and now rests in her family tomb, under heavy guard.

'A little while and I will be gone from among you. Whither, I cannot tell. From nowhere we came, into nowhere we go. What is life? It is the flash of a firefly in the night. It is the breath of a buffalo in the wintertime. It is the little shadow which runs across the grass and loses itself in the sunset.'

Crowfoot, c.1830 – 1890. The Indian name of the chief of the Blackfoot First Nation was Isapo-Muxika. He was born near Belly River in what is now Alberta, Canada. He probably first led a war party at 15 years old, when he rode to avenge his older brother's death by the Snake Indians. With his chiselled features and noble demeanour he made a striking figure and quickly earned a reputation for bravery in battle. Crowfoot discouraged tribal warfare and steadfastly refused to join rebellions against the North West Mounted Police and Canadian government. He died of pneumonia, surrounded by his tribe.

THE LAST POST

Spies, Soldiers and Revolutionaries

'This is a hell of a way to die.'

General George S. Patton, 1885 – 1945. Having survived the two World Wars, Patton was badly injured in a traffic accident and died two weeks later in hospital. He had been wounded in France during World War I and as commander of the US army had earned loyalty from his troops during World War II by leading from the front and making powerful and inspirational speeches. Following the war, he became something of a folk hero, partly inspired by his forceful personality. At his request, he was buried alongside his men and laid to rest at the American Cemetery in Hamm, Luxembourg.

....

'Death is nothing, nor life either, for that matter. To die, to sleep, to pass into nothingness, what does it matter? Everything is an illusion.'

Mata Hari, 1876 – 1917. The most notorious female spy was born Margaretha Geertruida Zelle in the Netherlands. Her father was a Dutch shopkeeper and her mother Javanese. Zelle later took the stage name Mata Hari, which meant 'the eye of the day'. Not only did she become a renowned exotic dancer, but was a talented linguist, highly intelligent and extremely attractive. She was dancing in Paris when World War I broke out and questioned about her German contacts by British forces. She claimed to be spying for the French and with a lack of evidence either way, the British released her. In 1916 she was arrested and tried in Paris for spying against France. She was found guilty and taken to Vincennes for her execution, where she made her last speech to a nun. Faced with her executioners, she refused a blindfold (and a priest) and blew the firing squad a kiss. Her body was used for medical research.

'France, army, Josephine.'

Napoleon Bonaparte, 1769 – 1821. The French general who became the first emperor of France may have been stating his priorities in order of importance. Following his defeat by the British at Waterloo, Napoleon was imprisoned on St Helena, an isolated island in the South Atlantic Ocean. He died there of a stomach disorder, which may have been cancer, although some have speculated that he was poisoned with arsenic.

He is widely considered one of the greatest political and military leaders and an innovator in military training as well as social organization. He married Josephine de Beauharnais in 1796 but had his marriage annulled in 1810 to wed the daughter of the emperor of Austria.

....

'I pray you to bear me witness that I meet my fate like a brave man.'

Major John André, 1750 – 1780. Born in London, to Swiss and French parents, André travelled to the United States, serving with British forces and was caught up in the American War of Independence. It was to André that Benedict Arnold offered to defect and with whom he carried out negotiations. When André was caught behind enemy lines, Arnold provided him with civilian clothes and false papers to aid his escape. André also carried Arnold's revelation of West Point's defences and when apprehended by American forces, these implicated both men, triggering Arnold's escape to Britain. André, however, caught in civilian clothes on American territory was treated as a spy rather than a prisoner of war and sentenced to death by hanging.

'Let me die in the old uniform in which I fought my battles for freedom. May God forgive me for putting on another.'

General Benedict Arnold, 1741 – 1801. Born in Connecticut, Arnold became a general for the Continental Army during the American War of Independence. Following the war he became a spy for the British. He had planned to surrender his command of West Point in New York to the British forces but the plan was discovered. Arnold escaped to London, where he died some years later. In the United States his name has since become synonymous with treason.

'Hurrah for anarchy! This is the happiest moment of my life!'

George Engel, 1836 – 1887. This German-born socialist and union activist was sentenced to hang for planting a bomb in Chicago. He had been involved in protests to limit the working day to eight hours but during one of the demonstrations, police had fired on the crowd and killed four men. At a subsequent rally, a bomb was thrown at the police, killing eight men and wounding many others. The police opened fire on the crowd killing an undisclosed number and wounding more than 200. Although several witnesses identified the bomber as Rudolph Schnaubelt, he was released without charge, prompting rumours that he was an *agent provocateur* in the authorities' service. Police then arrested several immigrants, including Engel, even though he had been at home on the night in question. Numerous witnesses attested that none of these men had thrown the bomb but the trial was unfairly slanted against them and they were found guilty. George Engel delivered his final speech on the gallows.

'They couldn't hit an elephant at this distance....'

General John Sedgwick, 1813 – 1864. Born in Connecticut, Sedgwick studied at West Point and began his military career fighting the Seminoles and forcing the Cherokee Nation from Georgia. At the outbreak of the American Civil War, he joined the Union, earning promotion and a reputation for bravery. He became both widely admired by his superiors and loved by his men, who called him 'Uncle John'. At the Battle of Spotsylvania Courthouse, Sedgwick was directing the artillery and troop placements. He paused to admonish his men for ducking down to avoid the enemy rifles. So confident was he of their safety that he resolutely remained standing – and was fatally shot through the face. He became the highest ranking casualty of the Civil War.

'Shoot straight, you bastards! Don't make a mess of it!'

'Breaker' Morant, 1864 – 1902. Despite being court-martialled for war crimes, this Australian soldier continued giving orders to the end, even to his own firing squad. Harry 'Breaker' Harbord Morant was born in Somerset, England. He moved to Australia in 1883 and settled in Queensland. He earned the 'Breaker' part of his name through his daring ability as a horseman. He also had a reputation as a charismatic womanizer, drinker and writer of popular ballads. Whilst fighting for the British in the Boer War, Morant was convicted of shooting a group of prisoners who had surrendered to his troops. The true circumstances of these events are still disputed, as are Morant's last words. Another version has it that he asked for his blindfold to be removed and once he was able to see, told the firing squad 'Be sure and make a good job of it.'

137

'Now, why did I do that?'

Major-General, Sir William Erskine, 1770 – 1813. So said Erskine immediately after jumping out of a window. He served in the British Army and represented Fife in the British Parliament. When Erskine was sent out to Portugal to fight in the Peninsular War, the Duke of Wellington remonstrated that he was a madman. 'No doubt he is sometimes a little mad,' replied the officials, 'but in his lucid intervals he is an uncommonly clever fellow...' Unfortunately, some of the decisions he made during his irrational periods claimed the lives of many men under his command. After a series of disasters, Wellington managed to manoeuvre Erskine to a position where he could do less damage. Eventually, he was declared insane and dismissed. He committed suicide by jumping out of a window in Lisbon.

....

'I know you've come to kill me. Shoot, coward, you are only going to kill a man.'

Che Guevara (pictured), 1928 – 1967. Ernesto 'Che' Guevara was born in Rosario, Argentina and studied medicine before embarking on a trip around South America. The poverty and inequality he encountered on his travels reinforced his Marxist ideals and generated a revolutionary zeal in him. He joined Fidel Castro's forces during the Cuban revolution and unsuccessfully tried to export the Cuban ideals to Bolivia. It was in Bolivia that he was captured and executed by the Bolivian Army. Although he has become the embodiment of a youthful, revolutionary figure, with his iconic image adorning countless T-shirts, he showed a ruthless, cold-blooded streak in the execution of political prisoners in Cuba.

'Let us cross over the river and rest under the shade of the trees.'

General Thomas 'Stonewall' Jackson, 1824 – 1863. Stonewall Jackson fought for the Confederacy under General Robert E. Lee during the American Civil War. Jackson was considered a hero for his service in the Mexican-American war and was promoted through the ranks. Following the Mexican war, he left the military and taught artillery tactics but returned to combat during the Civil War. His bravery and strategic skill on the battlefield brought him further promotions. Jackson was wounded by friendly fire during the Battle of Chancellorsville and his arm was amputated. He died several days later of complications and was buried in Lexington.

....

'Waiting are they? Waiting are they? Well – let 'em wait!'

Ethan Allen, 1738 – 1789. The American Revolution militia leader had initially fought against the British until captured and imprisoned for a while in England. However, when the Continental Congress refused to recognize Vermont's independence as a state, he entered into negotiations with British forces. His memoirs describing his military adventures became widely read in America. Allen died at his farm in Vermont, after suffering an apoplectic fit. His last comment was made in response to the doctor who told him that the angels were waiting for him.

'I do not have to forgive my enemies. I have had them all shot.'

Ramón María Narváez, 1800 – 1868. The 19th-century Spanish aristocrat and general had an unequivocal reply to his priest's query. He was also the first Duke of Valencia and a politician who led the government of Spain following his part in a coup.

....

'Don't let it end like this. Tell them I said something.'

Pancho Villa, 1878 – 1923. Born Doroteo Arango in the Mexican town of Durango, Villa began life as a poor farmer. At the age of 16, Villa shot the local hacienda owner for sexually harassing his 12-year-old sister. After escaping prison he became a bandit, gaining popular fame for robbing the rich and giving to the poor. Arango then changed his name to Francisco 'Pancho' Villa and eventually joined a rebellion against the Mexican dictator. Eventually, he formed his own band of revolutionaries who fought other rebel groups as well as U.S. forces on American soil. He became a folk hero in Mexico for his championing of the poor and downtrodden but also made many enemies. Although he had retired from revolutionary life, he was assassinated in Parral, Mexico in a well-organized hit and his killers were never caught.

POLICE DEPT.

DES PLAINES, ILL.

78-4621 2-21-78

THE END
OF THE
SENTENCE

Convicts and Criminals

'Well, gentlemen, you are about to see a baked Appel!'

George Appel, ? –1928. Appel was convicted of killing a police officer and robbery in New York City and sent to the electric chair. Just before the switches were thrown, he also joked, 'Damn, no power outage!'

....

'Hey fellas! How about this for a headline for tomorrow's paper: French Fries!'

James French, 1936 – 1966. Having received a life sentence for murder, French reportedly preferred to die than spend the rest of his years in jail. However, he was too afraid to kill himself, so strangled his cellmate instead, hoping to impel the authorities to end his life for him. They complied and executed him in the electric chair.

....

'Gentlemen, this is an educational project. You are about to witness the damaging effect electricity has on wood.'

Frederick Wood, 1912 – 1963. Wood was convicted of three murders during his lifetime and finally sentenced to the electric chair at Sing Sing prison in New York.

'Wow...that is awesome.'

Richard Cobb, 1984 – 2013. When asked whether he had any last words the rapist and murderer had given a rambling statement, ending with the comment, 'I hope that anyone who has negative energy towards me will resolve that. Life is too short to harbour feelings of hatred and anger. That's it warden.' However, as the lethal injection took effect, the prisoner raised his head from the gurney and looked towards the warden. In a loud and sarcastic voice, Cobb proclaimed, 'Wow! That is great. That is awesome! Thank you, warden. Thank you f*****g warden!' With that, he collapsed into unconsciousness and was pronounced dead some 15 minutes later.

....

'I don't care if I live or die. Go ahead and kill me.'

Jeffrey Dahmer, 1960 – 1994. Dahmer killed 17 young men over the course of 13 years; many of them in his grandmother's basement. He often kept body parts as mementoes or trophies and photographed the victims at different stages of the murder. The first police to search his home found a human head and three bags of human organs in his fridge. The jury declared him guilty and sane on all counts and he was sentenced to 15 consecutive life terms (around 950 years). Dahmer seemed repentant of his crimes, saying he was sick and professing relief that he would not cause any more suffering. He appeared to settle into prison life well but after only two years' incarceration, a schizophrenic prisoner killed him by smashing in his skull with a blunt instrument.

'You got me.'

John Dillinger (pictured), 1903 – 1934. Part of a violent gang of thieves who terrorized the Midwest during the Great Depression, Dillinger was ambushed by FBI agents and shot several times as he tried to escape. The 'Public Enemy Number One' began his criminal career with petty childhood thefts. At around 21 years old, he was jailed for a botched robbery. Whilst in prison, Dillinger refined his criminal education, acquiring skills from seasoned jail-mates and making friends with future gang-members. Two of these gangsters sprung him from jail and they headed to Chicago where they embarked on a bank-robbing spree which would only conclude when they were finally arrested. Their notoriety was tinged with an element of glamour, as stories about their exploits circulated among the public. On one occasion, they pretended to be a film crew making a movie about a bank robbery, as cover for actually robbing the bank. However, they left a trail of dead bodies in their wake, making them a priority target for the police and were all eventually arrested. Dillinger managed to slip free yet again and set to work with a new gang, which included Baby Face Nelson. Embarked on yet another crime spree, Dillinger's notoriety, growing along with the reward money, made it increasingly difficult for him to operate. Finally, he was betrayed to the FBI by an acquaintance. It was reported that a crowd gathered around his body and dipped their handkerchiefs and clothing into his blood as souvenirs.

'Well, nobody's gonna be shooting at me.'

Lee Harvey Oswald, 1939 – 1963. The suspected killer of President Kennedy had defected to Soviet Russia after serving in the U.S. Marines. He moved back to the United States with his Russian wife and their baby son in 1962 and took a job at the Texas School Book Depository in Dallas. Witnesses claimed that on the afternoon of 22 November 1963 they saw Oswald on the sixth floor of the depository, holding a rifle. As President Kennedy's motorcade passed the building, three shots were fired. Two of them hit the president, who was declared dead at hospital soon after. Oswald was seen again as he left the book depository. When confronted by a policeman, he allegedly shot the officer dead but was arrested later in the day. On 24 November, Oswald was being transferred from police headquarters to the county jail. At the centre of a scrum of police and news reporters, Oswald was handcuffed to Detective Leavelle, who joked with him, saying 'Lee, if anybody shoots, I hope they're as good a shot as you are.' Oswald laughed, saying that no one would shoot at him. Within seconds, a gunman emerged from the melee and fired straight at Oswald. The killer was Jack Ruby, a nightclub owner who claimed to act out of pity for the president's wife but his mob connections made his motives suspect and fuelled conspiracy theories which have proliferated around Kennedy's assassination. Oswald died on arrival at the same hospital that only two days earlier had fought to save President Kennedy's life.

'God bless America. God bless everyone. Let's do this damn thing!'

Mark Stroman, 1969 – 2011, was executed in Texas for shooting dead three people he thought were Muslim, following the 9/11 attacks. The only surviving victim of his rampage spearheaded the attempts to stay the death penalty, despite losing one eye in the assault.

....

'You guys doin' that right?'

Stanley 'Tookie' Williams, 1953 – 2005. The co-founder of *The Crips*, a Los Angeles street gang, Williams was convicted of four murders and two counts of robbery. During his first few years on death row, Williams assaulted guards and other inmates. After two years in solitary confinement, however, Tookie underwent a transformation as he turned to religion and away from violence. Despite his public contrition and anti-street gang work, his appeals against the death sentence were continually refused. His final plea was rejected by State Governor Arnold Schwarzenegger and Williams was executed by lethal injection at San Quentin Prison. Witnesses reported that the execution process seemed unusually protracted, as the nurse appeared to have difficulty inserting the needles into Tookie's arm.

'Kiss my ass! You'll never find the rest!'

John Wayne Gacy, 1942 – 1994. Known as the 'Killer Clown', Gacy was convicted of the rape and murder of 33 men, although it was widely suspected he had killed more. He was executed by lethal injection in Illinois.

....

'Is it safe?'

Dr William Parker, 1824 – 1856. The ironic last words of the condemned convict as he stepped onto the gallows. The killer known as the Prince of Poisoners and the Rugeley Poisoner was tried for only one murder (using strychnine) but suspected of at least eleven more victims, including his wife, four of his children, a brother and his mother-in-law. The debt-ridden doctor had repeatedly insured the lives of family members, only for them to die suddenly. He was hanged outside Staffordshire Gaol in front of an audience of more than 30,000 people. He remained in the popular imagination for a long time after his death and his effigy was displayed in Madame Tussaud's Chamber of Horrors for over a century.

'I'd like to be in hell in time for dinner.'

Edward H. Rulloff, 1819 – 1871. The educator and swindler was hanged for the murders of his wife and daughter. His was the last public hanging in New York.

....

'I did not get my SpaghettiOs, I got spaghetti. I want the press to know this.'

Thomas J. Grasso, 1960 – 1995 was clearly unhappy with his last meal. One Christmas Eve, Grasso had strangled an 87-year-old woman with her Christmas tree lights and robbed her house. The following year, he killed an 81-year-old man staying in the same boarding house. Grasso was given a 20 year to life sentence in New York, which does not have the death penalty. However, he was then extradited to Oklahoma to answer for the first murder. Capital punishment was practised in Oklahoma and the death penalty imposed. The two states then engaged in a complex legal tussle for the fate of the prisoner. Meanwhile, Grasso made it clear that he preferred to die, halting each of his appeals. He was eventually executed by lethal injection in Oklahoma.

'Yes, I would just like to say I'm sailing with the rock and I'll be back, like Independence Day with Jesus. June 6, like the movie. Big mother ship and all. I'll be back, I'll be back.'

Aileen Wuornos (pictured), 1956 – 2002. Wuornos confessed to the murder of six men, saying she had picked them up whilst working as a prostitute on the highway and then shot them after they attempted to assault her. She received one death sentence for each murder. Billed as 'America's first female serial killer', Wuornos sold the movie rights to her story and was the subject of several books and documentaries.

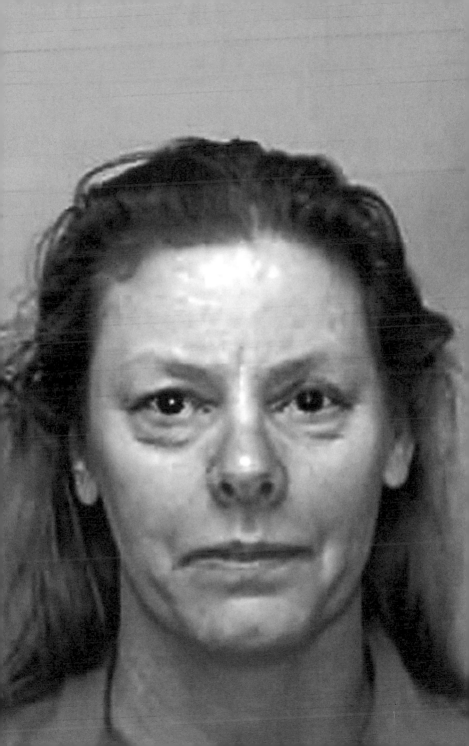

'Hurry up, you Hoosier bastard; I could kill ten men while you're fooling about!'

Carl Panzram, 1891 – 1930. The unrepentant American serial killer had been repeatedly jailed for theft where he compounded his crimes by violently attacking the prison guards. Panzram was a walking catastrophe, describing himself as 'rage personified'. He indulged in arson and vandalism and would rape his male robbery victims purely to humiliate them. In 1920, he embarked on a murderous spree, targeting sailors he found drinking in New York bars. He would encourage them to get drunk, then rape and shoot them and throw their bodies into the river. According to his own account, he killed ten men this way. Panzram then travelled to Angola, Africa where he claimed to have killed several people. On his return to America, he raped and murdered two young boys and killed five more men. He was eventually arrested for burglary but while in custody he confessed to murder. Panzram began to write his autobiography, in which he admitted to 21 murders along with countless burglaries, arsons and rapes. Initially sentenced to 25 years, after he battered a prison foreman to death with an iron bar, he received the death sentence. When anti-death penalty groups tried to appeal on his behalf, he threatened to kill them, too. On mounting the gallows, Panzram spat in the hangman's face saying, 'I wish the entire human race had one neck and I had my hands around it!'

'If any of you have a message to give the Devil, give it to me quick – I'm about to meet him!'

Lavinia Fisher, 1793 – 1820, and her husband were sentenced to hang for a series of murders in Charleston, South Carolina. John Fisher cringed and begged forgiveness but Lavinia was made of sterner stuff. With the noose around her neck, she addressed the assembled crowd, then threw herself from the scaffold, completing the executioner's task.

'I'll be in hell before you start breakfast – let her rip!'

Tom 'Black Jack' Ketchum, 1863 – 1901. This was the declaration from criminal Ketchum as he stepped onto the gallows. The Texas born train robber and member of Butch Cassidy's Hole in the Wall gang was sentenced to hang for his notorious crimes. Unfortunately, the gallows drop was too long for a man as heavy as Black Jack and as the rope snapped taut; the noose cleanly severed his head from his body, releasing torrents of blood from the gaping neck. Ketchum was just as dead but it provided a grisly show for the observers, many of whom turned away from the bloody spectacle. A less dramatic epilogue from the unlucky Ketchum was reported as, 'Goodbye. Please dig my grave very deep. All right, hurry up.'

'I'd like to thank my family for loving me and taking care of me. And the rest of the world can kiss my ass!'

Johnny Frank Garrett, 1963 – 1992. Garrett was convicted of the rape and murder of a 76-year-old nun at her convent in Amarillo on Halloween night. He was only 17 years old when the crime was committed. Many believed Garrett was insane after suffering terrible childhood abuse. Several institutions, including Amnesty International, the nuns from the victim's convent and even the Pope, petitioned against his death sentence. Although Garrett won a reprieve from the State Governor, this was overruled by the Board of Pardons and Paroles and he was executed in Texas by lethal injection.

....

'Cheerio.'

Antonio Mancini, c.1902 – 1941. The British gang leader was the first victim of Chief Executioner Albert Pierrepoint. Mancini had been convicted of killing a rival gangster in the West End of London and was executed at Pentonville Prison.

'You can be a king or a street sweeper but everyone dances with the Grim Reaper.'

Robert Alton Harris, 1953 – 1992. Born into a violent and abusive alcoholic family, Harris began getting into trouble with the law from an early age. At 25, he and his younger brother Daniel stole a car from two 16-year-old boys to carry out a bank robbery. The brothers took the boys to a secluded lake where Robert shot them both. The Harris brothers then returned to town but were caught less than an hour after the bank robbery. In a grim coincidence, an arresting officer was the father of one of the teenage boys who had been shot by the pair. The unfortunate policeman was unaware at the time that anything had befallen his son. Daniel Harris was found guilty of kidnapping and sentenced to six years' imprisonment, while Robert was convicted of two counts of murder and kidnapping and sentenced to death. He was executed in the gas chamber of San Quentin Prison in California and his last words were a misquotation from the film *Bill and Ted's Bogus Journey*.

'Ah well, I suppose it has come to this. Such is life.'

Edward 'Ned' Kelly, 1854 – 1880. Born in Victoria, Australia to an Irish convict father, Kelly was seen as either a folk hero and Australian icon or a selfish, cold-blooded murderer. After killing three policemen, Kelly hid out in the bush with his gang, making forays into the cities to rob banks. When police finally captured him, he was wearing homemade armour and a helmet. He was hanged in Melbourne.

'Tell my mother I died for my country. I thought I did it for the best. Useless, useless...'

John Wilkes Booth (pictured), 1838 – 1865. Booth made his acting debut at the age of 17 and with his talent and good looks he became an instant hit. However, a respiratory illness cut short his dramatic career and Booth turned his efforts towards supporting the pro-slavery movement, in opposition to abolitionists such as Abraham Lincoln. Putting his performing skills to further use, he spied for the Confederates during the American Civil War. He later became involved in a plot to kidnap President Lincoln but the scheme failed and Booth became increasingly frustrated. He resolved to take more dramatic action and, on 14 April 1865, he shot the president dead during a performance of *Our American Cousin* at a theatre in Washington DC. Immediately after the assassination, Booth jumped onto the stage crying '*Sic semper tyrannis!*' (Ever thus to tyrants!) and 'The South is avenged!'. Unfortunately for Booth, as he jumped back down, he broke his leg, which rather hampered his escape. He made it as far as Virginia, where he and his co-conspirators were found hiding in a barn. Although shot by the investigators, Booth still refused to surrender, so they set fire to the barn to force him out. He finally emerged, badly burned and died of his injuries shortly after.

ISBN: 978-1-909284-12-8

RW Press Ltd
www.rwpress.co.uk
RWPress@live.co.uk